PRAISE FOR THE BOOK

"In *The Tao of Twin Peaks*, William Dickerson evokes the three faces of Dale Cooper as he summons a trio of personas to tussle with the richest, most complex show in TV history. Dickerson the artist, academic and stoner-philosopher blend together—sometimes in the same paragraph—into a kind of tulpic voice that, like Lynch's masterwork, leaves us swimming in a sea of quiddity, exploring islands of ideas both symmetrical and jagged. Eventually, you'll look up from his volume's pages and ask yourself: WHAT YEAR IS THIS?"

   —Nick Braccia, author of *Off the Back of a Truck: Unofficial Contraband for the Sopranos Fan*, Co-Creator of Shudder's *Video Palace*

"William Dickerson uses his scholarly acumen as a storyteller and deeply analyzes David Lynch's worldbuilding and finds meaning behind the subtext of Lynch's gospel. With great eloquence and respect to both the material and reader, Dickerson explores character balance and their duality, pointedly revealing that everything has a significant purpose in the world of Lynch. This book is for diehard fans of David Lynch and those newly introduced to his iconic work."

   —Sadie Dean, Editor, *Script Magazine*

"In *The Tao of Twin Peaks*, William Dickerson sheds new light on the famously enigmatic series that has captured generations. Dickerson lifts the curtain, sharing key insights and offering observations much as a classical art scholar analyzes a Renaissance painting. The book offers deep cuts into the philosophy and emotional landscape of Lynch & Frost's ethereal town. Every era of *Twin Peaks* is covered here; Dickerson unlocks many a mystery and provides new interpretations. *The Tao of Twin Peaks* is a must-have for *Twin Peaks* enthusiasts."

   —Tony Wolf, writer/artist, *The New York Times & The Believer*

WILLIAM DICKERSON

"For all David Lynch fans craving more, William Dickerson delivers a necessary dose of pie, donuts, and damn good coffee for the doppelganger's soul. *The Tao of Twin Peaks* deftly explores how Lynch's themes encompass every aspect of the show's art and craft. Whether you're reflecting on your experience of watching the series or preparing to dive into the pit of scorched motor oil, this book is the perfect companion for you."

—Robert Kraetsch, Adjunct Professor of Cinematography,
American Film Institute

"In this enchanting tribute to *Twin Peaks*, Dickerson takes us on a vivid journey through Lynch's surrealist style, decoding the imagery like no one else can. His level of insight on Lynch is unmatched."

—Jeffrey Michael Bays, author of *Suspense with a Camera: A Filmmaker's Guide to Hitchcock's Techniques*

THE TAO OF TWIN PEAKS

THE MEANING BEHIND DAVID LYNCH'S HIT TV SERIES

WILLIAM DICKERSON
Illustrated by GILBERT LEIKER

WILLIAM DICKERSON

Copyright © 2025 by William Dickerson

Editor: Jane Gould
Book Layout and Illustrations: Gilbert Leiker
Cover Art: William Dickerson and Gilbert Leiker
Additional Graphic: Freepik

Kettle of Letters Press
New York, NY

All rights reserved. No part of this book may be reproduced, distributed, or transmitted in any form or by any means, including photocopying, recording, or other electronic or mechanical methods, without the prior written permission of the author.

This publication is not affiliated with *Twin Peaks*, Lynch/Frost Productions, any film or television studio, production company, or record label. This is a work of academic analysis.

ISBN: 9780985188696

DEDICATION

For Judge Thomas A. Dickerson and David Lynch

WILLIAM DICKERSON

CONTENTS

ACKNOWLEDGMENTS..........................Pg. 1

FOREWORD..................................Pg. 3

INTRODUCTION.............................Pg. 9
The yin and yang of *Twin Peaks*, and why balance is important to David Lynch

CHAPTER ONE
THE RED ROOM...............................Pg. 17
Why the Red Room is the key to decoding everything in *Twin Peaks*

CHAPTER TWO
THE RESURRECTION OF LAURA PALMER...........Pg. 43
How Laura Palmer transcends the shackles of a flesh and blood character

CHAPTER THREE
I'M NOT GONNA TALK ABOUT JUDY...............Pg. 67
The central question of *Twin Peaks* moves from "Who killed Laura Palmer?" to "Who is Judy?"

CHAPTER FOUR
EPISODE 8: THE RAPE OF SARAH PALMER..........Pg. 85
Episode 8: The origin of the show's themes of good and evil

CHAPTER FIVE
EPISODES 15-17: THE ERSATZ SHOW . . . . Pg. 117
Season 3's show within a show

CHAPTER SIX
FROM TWIN PEAKS TO ODESSA, TEXAS . . . . Pg. 147
Characters split in two: Agent Cooper/Mr. C and
Laura Palmer/Carrie Page

CHAPTER SEVEN
IS IT FUTURE OR IS IT PAST? . . . . Pg. 175
"What Year Is This?" How to interpret the end of *Twin Peaks: The Return*

EPILOGUE
IT IS IN OUR HOUSE NOW. . . . . Pg. 203
David Lynch's worldview and his pursuit of oneness

ENDNOTES . . . . Pg. 211

ABOUT THE AUTHOR . . . . Pg. 217

ACKNOWLEDGMENTS

This book would not have been possible without the help of my family, friends and colleagues throughout my years of filmmaking and writing about filmmaking. Thanks to my wife, Rachel, who has supported me through both the light and the dark, and to my son, Wyatt, who is a constant source of optimism. I also want to pay particular thanks to the teachers who have shared their experience and wisdom with me throughout the never-ending process of learning. I've been lucky enough to teach visual storytelling and share my experience with a new generation of aspiring artists, so I know firsthand the value of time spent in the classroom. I'm honored to be a teacher and consider this book an extension of my work in that realm.

I want to thank the faculty and administration of AMDA College and Conservatory of the Performing Arts and Hofstra University for their faith in me as a professor, most specifically, Jason Chaet and George Nicholas. I also want to thank a few of my professors who have left their indelible academic marks on me: Donn Cambern, Gill Dennis, D.C. Fontana, Edward Isser, Peter Markham, Jim McBride, Jack O'Connell, Rob Spera, and Steve Vineberg. I'd also like to highlight a few of my colleagues who continue to be steadfast artistic collaborators and cinematic confidantes: Rob Kraetsch, Dwight Moody, and Paul Yates. I'd also like to thank John Sandel and Tony Wolf, both of whom were extremely helpful during the proofreading process of this book, and Mike Civille for taking the time to write the foreword. To my editor, Jane Gould, thank you for doing amazing work on this book—it's always a distinct pleasure working with you—and to my layout designer, Gilbert Leiker, thank you for the beautiful illustrations and bringing this project to the next level.

I must also thank two people who, without them, this book would not have been written. First, my father, a wonderful writer who was not only the biggest source of encouragement when it came to my writing, but also the one who recommended *Twin Peaks* to me when I was just eleven years old. His recommendation went something like this, "William, there's this weird show on television, I think you might like it." And, second: David Lynch. David is the reason I became a filmmaker. His work is as much a part of me as the blood in my veins and I'm thrilled to be able to reflect on it.

Finally, thank you for reading.

FOREWORD

When I met William Dickerson ten years ago, a series of coincidences seemed determined to bring us together as professional colleagues and friends. I earned my PhD in American Studies in 2013, after spending years examining the ways in which American popular culture intersected with the country's social and political forces throughout the 20th century. As a filmmaker-turned-scholar, I narrowed much of my academic focus to Hollywood cinema, but also expanded to literature, advertising, art, and the culture of celebrity in the "American Century."

Will was already an accomplished filmmaker in 2013, having just released his terrific thriller *Detour*. He had been hired to teach directing classes at the New York Film Academy's campus in Los Angeles, and shortly thereafter, I was appointed Chair of his department. On an even more random note, my wife, who was a film executive at MarVista Entertainment, mentioned around this time that she had hired a sharp new director to helm one of their thrillers. It was Will.

From that point on, our paths would often cross—more out of choice than chance. I asked Will to screen *Detour* for our students and hosted the Q&A with him afterwards. I was impressed by Will's bulky director's binder for the MarVista film, and eagerly listened to his stories of directing Roddy Piper, a professional wrestling legend from both our childhoods. I sat in on Will's classes partly because it was my job, but I also found myself sticking around to listen as he methodically analyzed scenes for that day's lesson. Throughout these interactions, Will and I engaged with ease, whether we were talking about directing or debating new releases. Of course, I found out quickly that it was impossible to know Will and not talk about David Lynch. And why not? Lynch stands among other giants like Welles and Kubrick, whose maverick visions bled into the mainstream, despite creating works that tested the boundaries established by economically-minded studios.

What separates Lynch from other unconventional legends is *Twin Peaks*. The series would hold immeasurable influence on the television industry to come. When it debuted in 1990, primetime television was almost exclusively situational, with formulaic standalone episodes that allowed viewers to join in at any point. But Lynch opened the door to another possibility, challenging audiences to watch from the beginning and keep up week to week as the story unfolded. *Twin Peaks* blew apart the conventional wisdom that longform visual stories were confined to theatrical feature films or daytime soap operas, and it helped establish the layered, literary, and binge-worthy series structure that dominates today's "golden age" of television.

This is also what made *Twin Peaks: The Return* so fascinating. When it dropped in 2017, it was as if Lynch was checking in on the domain he helped create. However, *The Return* was uniquely in keeping with Lynch's career and all its unapologetic glory. Lynch chose not to rehash the 1990 version of the series, nor did he follow the familiar tropes that were becoming increasingly predictable in a television market oversaturated by hourlong dramas. In almost comical fashion. Lynch laid waste to expectations by resisting any pressure to "return" to *Twin Peaks* at all. Instead, he presented a whirlwind of scattered multiverses, new faces, and fractured characters, which frustrated some audiences (myself included), most likely to the amusement of its creator. For Will, though, it was vintage Lynch, begging to be pulled apart. He eagerly accepted the riddle presented by the director and embraced the opportunity to piece together the puzzle.

The result is the monograph that follows. When Will told me he was tackling Lynch's obscure saga, I was intrigued. I was not aware that he held the rigorous analytical abilities that populate these pages. Then again, I should not have been surprised. I knew all about Will's tireless commitment years ago, when I first saw him teach, or when I flipped through his elaborate 130-page director's look-book. His tenacity, when coupled with a fearless spirit, always fostered an unrivaled dedication to the task at hand. This sweeping exploration of *Twin Peaks* is no different, as Will's relentless determination and meticulous filmmaker's eye allows him to "see" things in ways that perhaps even lifelong scholars cannot.

Devotees of *Twin Peaks* and David Lynch will certainly delight in Will's exhaustive investigation. He offers a fresh look at episodes and overarching series themes, while synthesizing, integrating, and debating previous literature on the subjects. At the same time, this book will be an eye-opener for newcomers to the series and director. Will demystifies the intimidating mind of a creative juggernaut and carefully untangles the many narrative and thematic threads that Lynch simultaneously weaves. By the end of this book, readers will find that Will has accomplished a nearly impossible feat: he has made sense of *Twin Peaks*.

Just like when he directs, Will narrows the series down to recurring themes that clarify Lynch's complex opus and shows how the swarm of surreal dreamscapes interconnect both with narrative motifs and the postwar America in which Lynch grew up. This kind of research makes American Studies scholars giddy, but Will's approach is not overly intellectual, and casual fans will find his discoveries to be equally appealing. Over the last 20 years, I have read a lot of texts that revisit important cultural artifacts, and Will's contribution on *Twin Peaks* is essential, accessible, and on par with the best of them.

Most of all, *The Tao of Twin Peaks* made me want to revisit the series, armed with this newfound map of material to guide me through it all. Back in 2017, I admitted to Will that *Twin Peaks: The Return* had lost me around Episode 11. If a subset of critical and fan reviews are any indication, I wasn't alone. For some viewers, *Twin Peaks* may seem at times like an infuriating jumble governed by random chance and coincidence. But after reading Will's breakdown, I found myself pulled back into Lynch's phantasmagorical tornado, shaking my head simultaneously at his defiant storytelling and Will's detailed translation. Unlike the arbitrary events that brought Will and me together as friends, Lynch leaves nothing to chance and is in fully command of his world. This book confidently reveals his methodology. Read on, rewatch, and reward yourself.

—Michael Civille, PhD, Filmmaker and Film Historian

"Balance is the key. Balance is the key to many things. Do we understand balance?"

—The Log Lady

"What takes place between light and darkness, what unites the opposites, always has a share in both sides and can be judged just as well from the left as from the right…the only thing that helps us here is the symbol…with its paradoxical nature it represents the 'third thing.'"

—Carl Jung

WILLIAM DICKERSON

INTRODUCTION

David Lynch entered my life in 1990, when the original *Twin Peaks* aired. I happened to see one of the handful of episodes directed by Lynch. I was eleven years old. I had watched a lot of movies and seen plenty of television before then, but this was the first time I recognized a creative mind behind what I was seeing, someone who was in deft control of my emotions. What I was watching and absorbing awakened me into feeling something, something I couldn't quite articulate, but I knew was significant. It was at this moment that I realized I wanted to learn how to do whatever it was he was doing. Because of David Lynch, I set out on a journey to become a filmmaker. Steadily making films from that moment on, I later attended the American Film Institute Conservatory, Lynch's alma mater and the school he credited with starting his career. This was the place where he made *Eraserhead* in the horse stables on the outskirts of the school's property and I knew I had to go there. I am as diehard an admirer and fan of David Lynch and his work as it gets, and I know there are a lot of you out there who are too.

I'm lucky to have met David several times, through school functions and random run-ins—including a literal one: I almost drove my car into him and Laura Dern when they ran into the middle of Hollywood Boulevard while filming a scene from *Inland Empire*. I'm inclined to believe in "wavelengths" that tune similar people into similar worlds, and I think that's what most Lynch fans feel about their relationship to David and his work. This may also be the reason that a few years later, completely by chance, I ended up living across the street from his daughter Jennifer, with whom I've become friends. Parts of the introduction you're reading now were drafted on David's electric typewriter—an IBM Wheelwriter III—the one he used to co-write his episodes of the first incarnation of *Twin Peaks*. Jen was cleaning out her storage shed one morning and asked me if I wanted her Dad's typewriters, which he had given to her long ago. I accepted them with pleasure, of course, but also with a reverence I've rarely attributed to other objects I've received in my life. They had long since stopped working, but I found the one person in Los Angeles who still repaired typewriters and had them fixed.

Fast-forward several years. After making my film *No Alternative*, having my first child, Wyatt Cooper, and moving to New York, I rewatched the entire series of *Twin Peaks* and began writing about it. I've been working on this book for the past several years and I hadn't used the typewriters, but I knew I wanted to incorporate them into it somehow. I was skittish to even try using them, storing them in my basement until, finally, the task of writing this introduction presented itself. I thought the intro would be an appropriate place to utilize them. The consequences were both strange and bittersweet: the first time

I decided to use the *Twin Peaks* typewriter was the night before David Lynch passed away.

I was writing late into the night, making mistake after mistake and realizing how much I missed the absurd ease of such modern innovations as spell-check and the delete button. I'd crumble up papers and toss them to the floor, holding myself to the same level of perfection I believed Lynch held himself to when he used the machine. I even bought Wite-Out correction fluid—at a store, if you can believe it; I didn't think the product still existed. As I attempted to correct my mistypes, my eyes were drawn to the beige metal on the bottom right corner of the machine where there was a streak of smudged, long-dried Wite-Out, which Lynch probably used to correct his own mistakes. It reminded me that Lynch was a human being, just as I was, and I decided to stop for the night and start again the following day. But before I could, I got the news. David Lynch was dead.

Like most of his fans, I was devastated. Grief-stricken, really. Whenever I reflected on cinema as an art form, David Lynch was always at the forefront of my mind. This won't change for me, of course, but the fact that he is no longer here to catch ideas and manifest them through his work is a sobering one. On the day he died, I sat behind his typewriter and didn't type a word, letting the wordlessness of the device he wrote his words on wash over me. Words were a means to an end for David Lynch, but they weren't the thing itself. In fact, he harbored a deep mistrust of words, as evidenced by the nightmarish representation of letters in one of his earliest works, *The Alphabet*. In a *New York Times* tribute to Lynch following his death, his collaborator Kyle MacLachlan described his work as being "outside language, you are in the realm of feeling, the unconscious, waves." It is within this realm that Lynch's work resides, and I felt as though I were sitting within this same realm as I stared down at the keys unable to bring myself to use them.

No words could articulate what I was feeling, and that is precisely why Lynch found them limiting and didn't verbalize the meaning of his work. MacLachlan went on to write, "David didn't fully trust words because they pinned the idea in place. They were a one-way channel that didn't allow for the receiver." For Lynch, words were one-dimensional, and his work wasn't fully complete until the the viewer, listener, experiencer, *received* them. As I sat there, overwhelmed with sadness, I took comfort in knowing the words he wrote on these keys became part of something much more enduring and powerful and timeless than anything encumbered with mortality, or a typewriter ribbon, could achieve. They initiated a perpetual conversation between creator and viewer and, essentially, triumphed over death. They became *Twin Peaks*.

We see the world through stories and that has been essential to our species' survival. When we die, it's our stories that continue, whether they're passed down through family members or broadcast on network television. One can immerse ourselves in the need to make sense of life for more seconds, minutes, and hours than there are days, weeks, months, years...centuries. Stories truncate that process, that primal pursuit. Storytellers are searchers, detectives, and their consumers—the people reading or watching—are invited on the journey as a vicarious partner in this investigation. Stories allow us to view ourselves from the outside in. They remove the superego, the self, and therefore provide a window of opportunity to assess ourselves and our lives as objectively and non-judgmentally as possible. Stories are parables, using metaphor to help us structure our lives, be aware of the problems, and discover more efficient, meaningful, and universal ways to live.

Stories are also the basis of all ancient myths and religions. Then, of course, there's the story of *Twin Peaks*. *Twin Peaks* utilizes mythological and religious symbolism; however, it exists in a medium of three-dimensions, its story played out visually on the screen. Its impact is visceral, immediate, and modern.

If *Twin Peaks* is a belief system, then consider me a practitioner. There are few television shows that demonstrate the complex world-building and internal mythologies that draw viewers to *Twin Peaks*. I use the phrase "belief system" not to invoke the supernatural, though the series does delve into such phenomena in its storylines, but to stress the life the series has taken on outside the confines of the television set. It is a life that explores and, in my opinion, encourages a moral code that paves the way toward a comprehensive philosophy. As our world becomes increasingly binary—the perceived *good* and *bad* from tilted and every-increasingly extreme points of view—David Lynch's work confronts the metaphoric black and white, two juxtaposing worlds, in order to find a semblance of balance between them.

It is important for me to acknowledge the fact that David Lynch's following is legion and the array of theories about *Twin Peaks* are practically infinite. My intention is to neither discount, nor bolster, the theories of the show's viewers. I think it is important to respect and consider every viewer's opinion, as Lynch's work invites interpretation. Individual interpretations are unique to the interpreter. But even though our emotional connections to Lynch and his work may differ, they are similarly powerful— a testament to the filmmaker's ability to connect to his audiences. There may be a cult of Lynch, but the work itself is indicative of something more profound and enduring.

In this book, I hope to channel the spirit of David Lynch's work and convey the importance of *Twin Peaks* and its overarching themes. We often don't understand the themes, or lessons, of a story until the end. Lynch worked incredibly hard to keep his work a mystery; however, this does not mean he didn't know what his work was about. He knew exactly what he wanted to convey to his audience. The origins of the stories he told came from the air. He admittedly claimed to merely be a vessel for these ideas, and his expression of them was, subsequently, akin to a spiritual journey. He lived "the art life" and he lived it for a reason: he was compelled to do so. This journey can, and should, be experienced by his viewers and used to inform their lives as it informed his. As Lynch said in his memoir, *Room to Dream*, "Ultimately, each life is a mystery until we each solve the mystery, and that's where we are all headed whether we know it or not."

There have been many books and critical essays written about *Twin Peaks*. This book is different; it is a search for meaning for the most ardent fans of the show, as well as those who seek to understand the importance of art and stories in our lives—art as a spiritual guide. Before embarking on this journey, though, I encourage the reader to possess a basic preexisting knowledge of *Twin Peaks*, as this book explores the worlds of *Twin Peaks*, Seasons 1 and 2, *Twin Peaks: Fire Walk with Me*, and *Twin Peaks: The Return*. Such knowledge will provide the best foundation upon which to examine Lynch's themes and techniques.

I believe it's a worthwhile and, ultimately, insightful search for significance that I suspect their creator, David Lynch, wanted us to find.

> Thank you, David, for your words and images,
> music and weather reports, for my fondness
> of coffee and cherry pie, for your dedication
> to peace, and for changing the landscape of
> cinema--and my life--forever.
>
> --William Dickerson

WILLIAM DICKERSON

THE RED ROOM

Tao is a Chinese word that means "path." The deeper meaning of the word is connected to the philosophical idea that the universe operates in its optimal state when it is balanced, and it is through the Tao that we can find balance in the universe, harmonize with it, and thus achieve balance in our own lives.

Most all religions and spiritual belief systems implement a version of the Tao in their strictures; however, the idea of balance is of particular importance to Eastern theologies and belief systems. Eastern modalities literally appear throughout *Twin Peaks*, most notably through Special Agent Dale Cooper's affinity for Tibet and his use of Tibetan Buddhist beliefs in his methods of detective work.

Agent Cooper is introduced to us as a straight-as-an-arrow model of rational thought. It isn't until Episode 3 of the first season that we see the completely opposite side of Cooper's rationality: his Tibetan-inspired technique of deduction based on his intuition, which he came to learn through a dream. This is the first moment in *Twin Peaks* where we are confronted with the duality of its main character. The rational versus the irrational;

conscious thought versus unconscious thought.

The reliance on a rock-throwing game of chance to determine clues surrounding the murder of Laura Palmer is so outside the character of Agent Cooper, as we know him up to this point, that his behavior would seem entirely implausible if it weren't for his enthusiasm and assuredness and the fact that the game does produce a tangible lead in Leo Johnson. Reconciling the model of the rational with the model of the irrational seems impossible, but in *Twin Peaks*, it's not only possible, it's also emblematic of the model human being.

In Taoism, contrasting forces such as positive and negative, good and evil, are considered complementary as well as dichotomous to one another. Visually speaking, this idea is exemplified in the symbol of the yin and yang.

The symbol represents the natural dynamic balance between opposites, and with respect to the Tao, the potential for equilibrium between nature and human beings. It is used to convey an idea similar to the cause and effect of Karma, wherein every action generates a counteraction, which involves either the decreasing of the yin and increasing of the yang, or the increasing of the yin and decreasing of the yang, in equal proportions over time. For instance, if the darkness of the yin represents *evil*, then the brightness of the yang represents *good*. Nothing exists without its opposite; they devour each other, yet fulfill each other. Evil only exists in proportion to good, and good only exists in proportion to evil.

The references to the yin and yang in *Twin Peaks* are clear and significant, the most noticeable example residing inside the set of the Red Room. The Red Room is the key to understanding the theme of *Twin Peaks* and serves as the linchpin to the entire series. Its iconic black and white floor evokes the yin and yang, specifically how the dark and light are interconnected to each other, its zigzag chevron pattern directing the shades into and out of one another.

Chevron is an inverted V pattern: V and its opposite. This timeless pattern dates back to Ancient Egypt and is most clearly connected to Art Deco design, an aesthetic that is reflected in the chairs and lamps in the Red Room. The upward and downward angles are also reminiscent of electromagnetic waves. According to Chinese cosmology, the universe was born from a chaos of energy, a force that comprises the cycles of yin and yang, which shapes objects and lives.

The Red Room is where the chaos of the world of *Twin Peaks* is reconciled. It is the space where opposites confront each other and the yins and yangs decrease and increase in proportion to one another.

Agent Cooper is the primary character that inhabits the Red Room. He is the character the audience accompanies into this world. In the international version of the show, we're first introduced to the Red Room in the pilot. In the American version, that scene has been re-edited and not included until Episode 3 (or Episode 2, if you don't include the pilot in the episode count). For now, I will focus on the unabridged sequence in the international pilot, as I will be discussing the American television incarnation later in this book.

The first shot in the Red Room is a tilt-up from an upside-down reflection of an older Dale Cooper to the right-side-up version of him, sitting in a lounge chair. As the camera tilts up, the two versions of Cooper are framed between a green lamp depicting the planet Saturn, one ringed side facing down toward his reflection in the tabletop, the other facing up toward him. The two Coopers are split between this prop planet.

Opening and closing images are important visual markers for directors, and the good directors use them to plant the seed of a theme. It is clear that Lynch, from the very beginning of this sequence, establishes the idea of *two Coopers*—one Cooper being the inversion, the opposite, of the other. Lynch begins the Red Room sequence with a mirror image of the main character. The original incarnation of *Twin Peaks* ends with the mirror image of Cooper once again at the end of Season 2, except he is facing the opposite way, and in the mirror, he (and we as the audience) sees Bob reflected in it. The arc of Cooper's character is clear in the first two seasons—it reflects a journey from the good Cooper (the Good Dale) into the bad Cooper (Bob). The main character struggles to maintain the balance between these two parts of himself, only to succumb to the bad part—or, the

Jungian "shadow self"—by the end of the second season. Cooper remains out of balance, his darker side in control, for the next 25 years, until Season 3, *Twin Peaks: The Return*, wherein the Good Dale finally leaves the Red Room to battle for control over himself once again.

David Lynch referred to the Red Room as an "in-between place," and as the character Mike would say, he means it "like it is, like it sounds." This is the place where the light and dark sides of oneself face one another, where both sides of a person exist simultaneously, but are separate from one another. The Red Room is officially referred to as the Black Lodge in the series; however, it is also referred to as the White Lodge. The Black Lodge and White Lodge are one and the same, depending on which side of your self occupies it. Deputy Hawk invokes the legend of the

White Lodge, within which the Black Lodge exists as its shadow self, "every spirit must pass through there on the way to perfection. There, you will meet your own shadow self. My people call it 'The Dweller on the Threshold'... But it is said, if you confront the Black Lodge with imperfect courage, it will utterly annihilate your soul." The Red Room is the space between the two sides of yourself, within which these sides are reconciled.

This place is the line that waves its way through the middle of the yin and yang symbol, as it straddles both sides: oneself and one's doppelganger. It is the place where balance is restored.

This image of the two Coopers is of great import to this series, as this is what the plot of *Twin Peaks: The Return* focuses on. It is also important to note that the idea of the Red Room was not thought of until after the pilot was conceived and shot. David Lynch was contractually obligated to deliver the pilot as a stand-alone movie, with a closed ending, for broadcast overseas. As the story goes, in an effort to solve the problem of having to shoot an ending for it, he thought of the Red Room. Lynch had always envisioned the story of *Twin Peaks* as open-ended, the murder of Laura Palmer as a MacGuffin of sorts, a plot device that steered the show into the storylines of the supporting characters. He was not going to reveal the literal "who" in the question "who killed Laura Palmer" at the end of the international pilot; however, he wasn't going to leave the metaphorical *who* unanswered.

Just prior to the first Red Room sequence, Lynch introduces and, shortly thereafter, kills off two new characters: Mike and Bob.

It is fitting to meet these characters before the viewer is introduced to the Red Room because they are the manifestations of the forces of good and evil. David Lynch was a surrealist, and through his art, he communicated through symbols and visual metaphor embedded in dream logic. He reveals Bob as the killer of Laura Palmer, and this is not in any way misleading. Bob did kill Laura Palmer; the person who literally killed her was inhabited by Bob, in other words, by evil. Slyly, the surface of the scene plays out like a bad TV show, or B movie, with the bad guy declaring, "welcome to the killer's lair" and he "will kill again," and the good guy yelling "like hell" and shooting him dead. Lynch casts aside the literal, the surface, by mocking it, and in doing so, places all the importance on the non-literal, the metaphorical. This series is not about plot; it's about what's underneath the plot. It's not about the text; it's about the subtext.

In the poem that Mike recites before he leads Cooper to Bob in the basement of the hospital, he describes what the Red Room is:

Through the darkness of future past,
The magician longs to see,
One chants out between two worlds,
Fire walk with me.

The Red Room is a timeless space floating between the future and the past where one chants out "Fire walk with me." In Episode 11 of Season 3, Hawk explains that fire symbols can either be good or bad; it depends on the intention of the fire. Fire can be used to either create or destroy. In the hands of Mike, it can create; in the hands of Bob, it can destroy.

Mike evokes two other symbols of good and evil: the devil and God. Mike states, with a kind of pride, "I, too, have been touched by the devilish one, tattooed on the left shoulder, but when I saw the face of God, I was changed. I took the entire arm off. My name is Mike. His name is Bob." The spatial fact that Mike is above while Bob is below, in the basement, further solidifies the dichotomy between these two forces. Shortly after we are introduced to Bob, the malevolent character states, "head's up; tail's up," which is echoed when Mike asks Cooper for a "nickel." The symbolism is clear: Mike and Bob are two sides of the same coin. In fact, when Mike shoots and seemingly kills Bob, Mike dies himself. They are two sides of the same nickel; take one away, so goes the other. Thematically, Lynch is emphasizing balance, an equilibrium between good and evil. Good exists in opposition to evil, and evil exists in opposition to good. As a result, there must be a balance between them.

This sequence ends when Cooper says, "Make a wish," and the circle of candles are blown out. What does Cooper wish for? What is his purpose? His purpose is to investigate, and in this case investigate the murder of Laura Palmer. What is the ultimate goal of such an investigation? To restore the balance that was lost as a result of her murder. The scale has tilted toward the side of evil with the murder, and Cooper is there to tilt it back to the side of good. The death of Laura Palmer has knocked the lives of the people in this small town out of balance, but restoring such a thing is not so easy.

The title "TWENTY-FIVE YEARS LATER" appears on the screen, and then the first shot of the Red Room sequence, which I previously referenced, begins. Having just been introduced to the personifications of good and evil, Lynch cuts to the two sides of the same Cooper; a mirror image of the man himself, one side good, one side evil. That's how this visual language should be interpreted, as the idea of the two sides of Cooper manifest themselves literally in Season 3. It is quite revealing that the very first moment we are in the Red Room, we are introduced to the visual concept of two Coopers, and this is the place where these two Coopers exist.

In addition to Cooper, the other two characters that appear in the first Red Room sequence are the Arm and Laura Palmer, in that order. Lynch cements us in Cooper's point of view as he looks toward the Arm, a small man dressed in red moving backwards toward him from the corner, and then as he looks toward Laura sitting across from him. The audience is seeing the Red Room for the first time just as Cooper is seeing it, through a series of shots from his perspective—he is the vessel through which we experience these impressions.

As Cooper continues to hear the shuffle of the Arm's feet moving toward him, he turns and looks at him again. The little man spins around, grabs hold of a standing lamp and declares, "Let's rock," in a cadence that is created by filming the actor say the line phonetically backwards and then playing that performance backwards. This has the effect of a line that is pronounced forward, but sounds like it's being spoken backwards. Everyone in the Red Room speaks and physically moves like this, except for Agent Cooper, the outsider, if you will. He serves as the proxy for the audience.

When the Arm grabs the gold lamp, the top and bottom of the lamp are outside of the frame, making it appear as though it is simply a pole extending down into the floor and up into the ceiling. It's only until the first wide shot of the sequence that we understand it is a lamp. This detail along with his declaration of, "Let's rock," establishes a connection to Elvis Presley and the birth of rock and roll. Elvis had an enormous influence on Lynch and echoes of Elvis reverberate through the filmmaker's work.

On a podcast for KCRW, Lynch cited Elvis's "That's All Right (Mama)" as the song that has most influenced him, and it is no coincidence that he hired Chris Isaak—a man and musician who is, essentially, an Elvis doppelganger—to play the precursor to Special Agent Dale Cooper in his film *Fire Walk with Me*, who mysteriously disappears with the words "Let's Rock" left on his car's windshield in his wake.[1] The famous chorus of "Let's rock" is from the song, "Jailhouse Rock," and in the movie of the same title, a black and white striped-shirted Elvis grabs a gold pole extending from floor to ceiling as he shouts the chorus before sliding down it.

After Cooper absorbs these words from the Arm, Lynch finally cuts to a wide shot—a shot that's traditionally used to establish a location—of the entire space. The Red Room and its eclectic accoutrements are now clearly exhibited: black and white zigzag floor, red curtains for walls, curvilinear lounge chairs, side table with a green Saturn lamp, two standing torchiere lamps and a statue of the Greek goddess Aphrodite, who is also known as the Roman goddess, Venus. From the moment this sequence aired on television, the Red Room became iconic; we had never really seen anything like it. It seemed directly plucked from Lynch's subconscious and piped to us through the tubes in our televisions. However, all thoughts are informed by surrounding thoughts and experiences, and in the case of an art form as collaborative as filmmaking, such thoughts must be communicated to creative partners such as cinematographers, production designers, prop masters, and costumers. Lynch often remarked that his purpose as an artist was to stay true to the idea, and that also went for his collaborators. Each and every one of their decisions hinged on the same objective: stay true to the idea.

Longtime Lynch interviewer, Chris Rodley, once noted to Lynch in regard to the visual and audio indicators—symbols, if you will—in his work: "...at times it does seem as if you're delighting in teasing or mystifying the viewer." Lynch responded, emphatically: "No, you never do that to an audience. An idea comes, and you make it the way the idea says it wants to be, and you just stay true to that. Clues are beautiful because I believe we're all detectives."[2] With respect to the design of the Red Room, let's take a closer look at the creative decisions he and his collaborators made and decipher the clues they offer us.

As we continue our examination of the floor, it is important to recognize what came before. While this floor is often recognized as being associated with *Twin Peaks*, at least with respect to the visual mediums of film and television, it has been utilized before, even by Lynch himself. This floor was the same style of floor used in the lobby of Henry's apartment building in Lynch's first feature film, *Eraserhead*. It was also featured prominently in Jean Cocteau's 1950 film, *Orpheus*, inside of a room that serves as the gateway through which the main character passes into the underworld. Jean Cocteau was an avant-garde writer and director who practiced surrealist film techniques. The story of *Orpheus* is based on the Greek myth in which Orpheus travels to the underworld to rescue his dead wife and restore her to the world of the living. This, in essence, is the same objective of Dale Cooper's character throughout the series: he wants to 1) solve Laura Palmer's murder and, in doing so, preserve her memory; and 2) travel back into the past to rescue her from being murdered, which amounts to bringing a dead person back to life.

When Orpheus prepares to travel through his magical mirror and into the underworld, he must put on special gloves, and the manner in which Cocteau portrays this is backwards. Cocteau films the actor who plays Orpheus, Jean Marais, taking off these gloves, so that when he plays it in reverse for the audience, it creates the effect of the gloves being put on in forward motion, but presented in the most uncanny, supernatural of ways. This is precisely the way Lynch films his actors in the Red Room.

In Cocteau's film, Orpheus is a poet who gets the ideas for his poems from radio transmissions. He sits in his car, listens to the words being spoken to him from beyond, and writes them down as if they're his own. Ideas are transmitted through radio waves. This metaphor for the manner in which an artist generates or, more specifically, receives ideas is the same way Lynch said he came up with his ideas. He described his process as, "No idea, no idea, no idea, then boom! It's like, you could say, a big movie screen in your head, in your brain. This idea comes on the screen. And you see it, you hear it, you feel it, you know it, all at once, and then you go and write it down."[3] Ideas are not generated; they are received from the air. This is what Orpheus experiences in Cocteau's film.

When Lynch was asked by collaborator Kyle MacLachlan what his favorite part of *Twin Peaks* was, he narrowed it down to the Red Room, and then told his story of how the idea came to him. Lynch mentioned that he was under pressure to come up with an ending for the international pilot, and as he was leaning on a hot car, the idea came to him out of thin air. He also made a gesture, moving his hand down toward the back of his head, as though the idea descended from above.[4] Orpheus received his ideas from radio waves in his car and, in a sense, so did David Lynch.

The ideas—the inhabitants of the Red Room—are dancing atop the electromagnetic radio waves—the black and white zigzag floor—and are caught on film by Lynch and then transmitted to us through our television sets. It is no coincidence that Lynch's favorite part of the series is also the key to understanding the series.

The solution to a problem involving television was, in part, television itself. The set of the Red Room is the nightmarish circus version of our everyday living rooms. As the little man begins dancing, a stroboscopic light begins flashing from the corner; the one corner we can't see; the corner of the living room where the television typically sits, flashing its staccato light onto its viewers. On the other side of the television screen: the viewers. Not unlike the mirror in *Orpheus*, our television is the gateway into the underworld that is the Red Room.

In the mid to late 1950s, David Lynch and most kids around his age huddled around their television sets to watch rock and roll visually transmitted to them for the first time through *The Ed Sullivan Show*. When Elvis Presley first appeared on the show in 1956, it caused a sensation, so much so that in future appearances he was shot from the waist up to censor his thrusting pelvis from the eyes of innocent viewers.

For Lynch, art was inseparable from the medium through which the artist chose to communicate their ideas. In an interview with *The Los Angeles Times* about his art, Lynch said in regard to his paintings' frames, "I saw a Francis Bacon show in the '60s at Marlborough Gallery in New York, and he had his paintings framed this way [Bacon's paintings were mounted in outsized gold frames that were as much a part of the art as the paintings themselves]. I loved his paintings and the frames just put them through the roof."[5] Lynch then referenced the similarly large and elaborate frames that he built to house his own paintings at a recent exhibition: "The paintings will live in these frames. They are part of the thing."[6] In the same sense, so too is his television work; the TV itself is part of it. It's been widely recognized that *Twin Peaks* is a television show that is aware that it's a television show, which provided a lot of humor for the audience. It is a metafictional dimension that is alluded to through its show-within-a-show, *Invitation to Love*, which mirrors the real show's storylines in tongue in cheek fashion. When series co-creator Mark Frost was asked about the inclusion of this soap opera in the show, he said, "I think that watching television is a big part of people's lives in this country and you very rarely see that treated in television."[7] Television so permeated the creative process behind *Twin Peaks* that television itself became the solution to Lynch's problem of how to end the international pilot.

Toward the end of this first Red Room sequence, the Arm opines, "Where we're from, the birds sing a pretty song, and music is always in the air," and in the 50s, it was the sound of televisions reverberating these sounds throughout the living rooms, dens, hallways, and the open windows of the American home. This was before air conditioning and people kept their windows open a lot more than today. Perhaps it was the sound of the movie, *Jailhouse Rock*, that was in the air and Elvis singing the song, "I Want to Be Free," in which he describes looking out his window and seeing "a bird, way up in the tree."

Elvis performs it on a stage in front of floor-to-ceiling curtains—later colorized to a *Wizard of Oz-esque* green on VHS in 1988—and as the song continues, he expresses his desire to be as free as the bird he sees in the tree. These lyrics not only bring to mind one of the final shots in Lynch's film, *Blue Velvet*, specifically the robin framed through the window, but also the glass window of the television set, through which music begins to play and the little man dances in the room that's red.

Television was first introduced to the masses at the 1939 World's Fair in New York, which revolved around the theme, *The World of Tomorrow*. The fair burst with science fiction and space motifs. General Motors held an exhibit called Futurama that boasted a magical ride through time and space. Westinghouse buried the first "time capsule" in Queens to be opened in 6939, precisely 5,000 years later. However, most relevant to this writing is the fair's association with television. RCA released the invention as a consumer device to the public at this event, and Franklin Roosevelt was the first president to be filmed and broadcast on television speaking at the exhibition. Not only did television play a role in Lynch's upbringing and artistic sensibility, it gave birth to *Twin Peaks*. It is safe to say, there would be no *Twin Peaks* without it, of course.

The 1939 World's Fair and the birth of television are directly connected to the Red Room through its Saturn lamp prop. While the lamp, at first glance, may appear like a superfluous detail unrelated to the show's larger themes, it's important to note that this lamp was specifically made for, and sold at, the 1939 World's Fair. The lamp is likely one of the "Saturn" souvenir lamps the L.J. Houze Convex Glass Company designed exclusively for the fair, or a replica of it. It came in a variety of colors; however, the one featured in most of *Twin Peaks* is the frosted green version. Interestingly, it achieved this color through the use of uranium glass, a type of glass that contains uranium— enough to register background amounts of radiation with a responsive Geiger counter. In other words, the lamp is nuclear.

Nuclear weapons, specifically the atomic bomb, play a critical role in *Twin Peaks*. While the subject isn't touched on directly in the first two seasons, besides Sheriff Harry S. Truman's name and the mention of Mr. Tojamura being from Nagasaki, Season 3 hinges on the idea that Bob was born from the Manhattan Project's atomic bomb test in White Sands, New Mexico on July 16th, 1945 at 5:29 a.m. There is nothing more Lynchian than the pure white sands of this locale being blackened by a weapon of mass destruction. The year 1939 not only presided over the futuristic World's Fair, it also marked the start of the Manhattan Project. Roosevelt started work on the project by creating the Advisory Committee on Uranium, a group of scientists and military officials assigned to research the element's potential as a weapon.

The main objective of The Manhattan Project was to split the atom. Splitting atoms result in the release of energy. The heavier the atomic element, the higher the amount of released energy. Uranium is, notably, the heaviest naturally stable element on earth, consisting of 92 protons and 92 electrons, which, when split, produces an immense amount of energy. Its high number of neutrons allows nuclear fission to occur with ease. By controlling this reaction, uranium's energy can be harnessed in a way that creates safe nuclear power for people—or that can destroy cities, states, countries, and potentially, the world and the people in it. The dichotomy of nuclear power, the opposite purposes of life and death, correlates to Deputy Hawk's description of the fire symbol. Nuclear power can be used for *good*, or for *bad*; it depends on the *intention*.

Furthermore, the very nature of how nuclear power is created resonates with the very core of *Twin Peaks*. Splitting the atom is a metaphor for the dualism that *Twin Peaks* explores through its characters, its world and its fundamental themes. It is the two sides of the same coin, of Mike's nickel, but with devastating implications. When the plutonium atoms are split and the bomb explodes in White Sands, and three weeks later, the uranium-based "Little Boy" detonates over Hiroshima, the Atomic Age begins. The time period casts a dark shadow over the idyllic 1950s. Lynch grew up in a time when crouching under school desks during bomb drills was the norm and living with the threat of nuclear annihilation was as routine as drinking a bottle of Coca-Cola.

Mankind now had the power to destroy itself in the literal sense, and Lynch uses this phenomenon as the origin story for the antagonist, and resulting protagonist, of his television series. In Episode 8 of Season 3, we come to understand that Bob—*the evil that men do*—was born from the bomb blast. As a result, Laura Palmer—*the potential for man to do good*—was created as the antithesis to Bob; not the antidote, the antithesis. The evil that men do cannot be eliminated; however, it can be counterbalanced by the potential for good in people. Laura represents this potential. In other words, Laura is the yang to Bob's yin.

If we accept the splitting of the atom as the origin of this story, we must also recognize its similarities to the origin story of the world's largest religion: Christianity. In *The Book of Genesis*, God split *Adam*, creating Eve. But instead of living in peace together in the Garden of Eden, the pair are tempted by Satan and eat from the tree of knowledge, thus creating original sin. Scientists split the *atom*, and instead of using it to create, they used it to destroy, cementing modern man's original sin. The Fireman, aka the Giant, is the closest figure to a god in Season 3, as he creates Laura Palmer to counteract the birth of Bob. Throughout *Fire Walk with Me*, the only part of the *Twin Peaks* canon that explores the duality of Laura Palmer, we are presented with an individual who is split down the middle. She is both the madonna and the whore. Just as Frank Booth put his "disease" in Dorothy Valens in *Blue Velvet*, Bob has infected Laura Palmer through physical and mental rape. She struggles to reconcile the opposite parts of herself. In her final scene with James Hurley toward the end of the film, she tells him, "your Laura disappeared," before running off into the woods toward her impending death.

Laura Palmer struggles with being split apart throughout the movie, and this theme of division runs its course throughout the entire television series. The Red Room manifests this division, but on a scale that is both human and cosmic. When an atom is split, it produces energy through nuclear *fission*, the process that generates the energy for the atomic bomb. However, energy can also be produced through the process of nuclear *fusion*, in which two nuclei merge together, creating a unified nucleus. This generates the type of energy that creates stars; the sun was created through nuclear fusion, its core the result of this reaction. In Season 3, Laura Palmer's image is framed within a golden sun-like orb. Bob manifests himself within the darkness; Laura manifests herself within the light. And it's the light that exposes the darkness.

Nuclear fission is the exact opposite of nuclear fusion. The process of splitting versus the process of joining; two opposite manufacturers of energy that can either be used to destroy or used to create.

If we expand on this metaphor and imagine Laura as the sun, she lies in a class between a giant star and a red dwarf. *Giant* stars and *dwarf* stars exhibit an extreme difference in brightness, but share a similar temperature. The terms themselves reflect opposite attributes. Giant stars are tens, if not hundreds, of times brighter and larger than the sun, and red dwarfs are the dimmest and smallest of hydrogen-burning stars. In *Twin Peaks*, there is a distinction between the representatives of light and dark in the world of the Red Room. They are the Giant, aka the Fireman, and the little man, aka the Arm, who is depicted as a red dwarf. The parallels to these two opposite types of stars are evident, and Laura Palmer is caught between them. When the Sun eventually dies, it will become a giant and then shrink into a dwarf, before surrendering to darkness.

Mark Frost, who has admitted that Carl Jung influences his work, said that the Red Room is where beings encounter their *shadow selves*. This parallel universe is full of parallels and mirrors of parallels. At one point in the first Red Room sequence, we see the shadow of the planet Saturn revolve around the room behind the curtain. The Saturn lamp remains in place as its shadow revolves around it. Saturn is named after the Roman god of time—time continues to move beyond the curtain, but it is stopped inside the confines of the Red Room, its silhouette solidified within uranium glass, the *time bomb*.

Just prior to the revolution of Saturn's shadow, the Arm rubs his hands together in a contemplative fashion, creating what sounds like a Tibetan singing bowl being played. A singing bowl is played by rubbing the leather part of a wooden mallet in a circular motion against its outer metal edge. Visually, this motion creates a ring around the object; sonically, it creates a ringing sound that sustains. In Tibetan Buddhism, monks believe that singing bowls work to guide the body's cells into harmony with one another, as well as to promote the balance of energy inside the body. They believe that the ringing of the bowls can help tune the player into the sounds of the universe.

When we see the Arm in a wide shot rub his hands and create this sound, it's as though he is summoning the shadow of Saturn, which appears behind him as he rubs and the ring reverberates. The visual and audio ring of a singing bowl evokes the planetary shape of Saturn and thus corresponds to the appearance of Saturn's shadow. However, what can we make of the Arm's subsequent lines of dialogue, the good news about "that gum you like is going to come back in style," which seem to be sparked by a thought in his head the audience is not privy to? Or are we privy to it?

The shadow of Saturn beyond the curtain behind him seems to operate as an externalized thought projection; the Arm's head even moves in the direction of the shadow as it passes behind him. Immediately after the shadow has passed, the Arm smiles and states, "I've got good news," as though he has just received it. But what does Saturn have to do with gum?

The original working title of *Twin Peaks* was *Northwest Passage*, its Washington state locale a critical part to establishing the show's world and mysterious mood. One of the oldest and largest gumball machine companies is a company called Northwestern Gumball Machines, under the umbrella of the Northwestern Corporation. The company started in 1909 and in the 1930s grew to become the premier supplier of bulk vending equipment in America; its Model 60 gumball machine became the best selling bulk vending machine of all time.

Vending machines are a staple of modern Americana and convenience, both obsessions of David Lynch. One of the most popular of Northwestern Corporation's gumball machines was the Saturn 2000, which was a giant red, white, and blue rocket ship with a gumball dispenser at its base. The machine was released around the time of the height of rock and roll and there is a high likelihood that this machine, or other Northwestern machines, were a routine part of Lynch's childhood in the late '50s and early '60s.

The connection between space and gum is glued together through convenience, which as we see in *Fire Walk with Me*, is intrinsically connected to the Red Room, as it is above the "convenience store" where the evil entities from the Red Room often convene. Jung believed that universal truths could be understood in the collective unconscious through the use of symbols and *Twin Peaks* is chock full of them, like gum in a gumball machine.

By way of a more tangential example, for those who may have thought the atomic bomb origin story in Season 3 came too far from out of left field, we must consider Lynch's prior work; specifically, *Eraserhead*. Not only does the main character, Henry, have a framed photo of the atomic bomb hanging in his bedroom, a space with rather sparse décor, but the notable portrait shot of Henry, his hair backlit amidst a cloud of dust, is also reminiscent of the atomic bomb blast. This is the image that was used for the movie's poster, as it's quite powerful and meant to be. Henry, himself, is a ticking time bomb, his timer having started the moment he became a father. He, like most human beings, has the potential within him to kill his own child. It's a part of the *evil that men do*, an evil that Lynch links to atomic bomb imagery.

As we continue to deconstruct the design of the Red Room, the interstellar connection to Roman and Greek mythology is perhaps most clear with the inclusion of the statue of Venus de Medici. While less iconic than the Venus de Milo, the Venus de Medici happens to be one of the most copied statues in history, a characteristic that makes it a more appropriate object for the Red Room. Not only is the Red Room home to our shadow selves, this place literally manufactures copies, *tulpas*, of people, as we witness in Season 3. The question of what is reality and what isn't; which version of Cooper is the real version of Cooper—*which version of you is the real version of you*—is essential to the design of this place. The two identical torchiere lamps that bookend the sides of the two chairs, while a staple of the Art Deco movement, evoke ancient Roman torches. The lamps' symbolic connection to fire is also quite fitting for the room, and a twin set even more so. Additionally, the planet Venus is also commonly referred to as Earth's twin planet, as they are both very similar in mass and are neighbors to one another. However, the major difference between them is the fact that Venus rotates in the

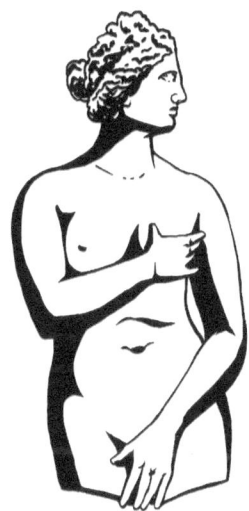

opposite direction; clockwise instead of counterclockwise, the way most planets spin. There is perhaps a connection between the backward rotation of the planet and the backwards-speak of the inhabitants of the Red Room, as one might consider Venus the upside-down version of Earth. The fact that in Season 2 the show makes clear that the door to the Black Lodge—aka the Red Room—opens every 20 years or so during the conjunction of Jupiter and Saturn is further evidence that space and its planets play important symbolic roles in understanding the deeper meaning of the show and its characters:

> **COOPER:** *Well, historically, Harry, when Jupiter and Saturn are conjunct, there are enormous shifts in power and fortune. Jupiter being expansive in its influence, Saturn, contractive. Conjunction suggests a state of intensification, concentration. What this indicates to me is the potential for explosive change, good and bad.*
>
> **TRUMAN:** *So when's the next conjunction?*
>
> **COOPER:** *Well, now, let's see. According to the ephemeris, the next conjunction is due January to June. My God, Harry. The door to the Lodge. That's when it's open. That's what the puzzle is telling us. It's telling us when it's gonna be open.*

The concept of expansion and contraction, as represented by these two planets during this rare, but routine, cycle further emphasizes Lynch's world of opposites and the necessity of balance between them.

Much like space itself, the timelessness of this red-curtained, black-and-white-floored living room, born of the mind of David Lynch, is wholly apparent. It is designed for the viewer to get lost inside of, as the characters that enter this place in the series are, in essence, lost. However, it's not been designed for its visitors to remain lost. That's what the symbols, the clues, are there for: to help us find our way out. They exist for us to find our balance.

Just as Agent Cooper says at the beginning of Season 1, "My dream is a code waiting to be broken. Break the code, solve the crime." Lynch has given his audience its mission.

WILLIAM DICKERSON

THE RESURRECTION OF LAURA PALMER

In *Fire Walk with Me*, the prequel film to the series that details the final days of Laura Palmer's life, the opening and closing images operate on numerous metaphorical levels. The film opens on an extreme close-up of television static, which creates a visual effect of rapidly moving black and white shapes bouncing around each other in seemingly random patterns. As the credits appear and disappear, the camera slowly zooms out, bringing the black and white particles into finer focus and ultimately revealing the television set on which they dance. Shortly after the words "Directed by David Lynch" appear on-screen, an axe comes hurling into frame and slams down onto the television, practically severing it in half as sparks flitter.

The fact that David Lynch literally takes credit for this off-screen person killing a television says a lot about his thoughts toward the medium at this time. In regard to network executives mandating that Lynch reveal who killed Laura Palmer, he said: "The thing that kills me is that the murder of Laura Palmer was never supposed to be solved. And the reason is that it's this beautiful little goose and that little goose is laying golden eggs and why would you kill this little goose? It's unreal. It's a huge sadness...a huge sadness. That mystery was sacred. It was the tree and the other ones were the branches. It is, like I said, a sadness."[8] Television forced Lynch to kill Laura Palmer's storyline by solving her mystery, but Lynch fights back, killing the television version of the show in order to resurrect Laura's storyline through cinema. The light of the movie projector will bring Laura back to life and that's where her mystery will live on.

The closing image of the film shows Laura Palmer inside the Red Room, Lynch's nightmarish living room, staring into flashing light. This image comes full circle from the opening image, as the light pitter-pattering against Laura's face resembles the way the light hits someone's face when it's emitted from a television screen. In other words, Laura is watching television. The movie begins with the viewer watching a television and ends with the main character watching a television. Laura is reacting to what she sees on the screen, and her reaction is one of bliss. I will explore this scene further, but in order to do so, we must first explore the death of Laura Palmer itself.

Fire Walk with Me, while tied to the original series, is very much its own separate work, and this has everything to do with Laura Palmer. The character of Laura Palmer in the television show was a device, plain and simple. She was the catalyst that sparked the entire series. Her murder brought Agent Cooper to *Twin Peaks*. Her murder brought the storylines of everyone else in town into the light. Her murder was the mystery that spawned countless other mysteries; at least, that's what was supposed to have happened. Lynch had intended for her murder, and the subsequent investigation, to fade into the background as the background stepped onto center stage. However, due to mounting public pressure, the network forced Lynch to maintain the show's focus on the investigation and reveal the murderer to the audience.

Laura Palmer was a force of nature inside the show, as well as outside of the show. Sheryl Lee, an aspiring actress with little experience at the time, was cast to play a corpse in the pilot episode of a television series. As it turned out, Lynch later discovered, Lee was an actress of immense talent. It was the combination of this discovery and the director's penchant for doppelgangers that led to the creation of Madeleine "Maddy" Ferguson, Laura's cousin who was also played by Lee. The only discernable differences between the two characters were her dark hair and glasses; but the intention was clear, she was a stand-in for Laura, a chance for the other characters in the show to interact with the dead. Perhaps Lynch created her as a way to satiate the public's appetite for Laura and keep the network off his back, or maybe he was just as obsessed with Laura as we all were and continue to be.

Laura Palmer was beyond everyone's control, even her creator's; her introduction to the world after her death gave birth to a life bigger than the show itself. Maddy provided a conduit through which the characters on the show could commune with Laura and confront, and relive, their memories of her. This is most certainly what led to her death at the hands of Leland Palmer, who relived his love and lust for, and ultimately the murder of, his daughter. She was a whiff of the past and, as such, her name alludes to the novel *A Remembrance of Things Past* in which French author Marcel Proust famously described how the taste of a madeleine cookie with a cup of tea triggered memories so vivid it was as though he was experiencing them again in the present:

No sooner had the warm liquid mixed with the crumbs touched my palate than a shudder ran through me and I stopped, intent upon the extraordinary thing that was happening to me. An exquisite pleasure had invaded my senses, something isolated, detached, with no suggestion of its origin. And at once the vicissitudes of life had become indifferent to me, its disasters innocuous, its brevity illusory—this new sensation having had on me the effect which love has of filling me with a precious essence; or rather this essence was not in me it was me. ... Whence did it come? What did it mean? How could I seize and apprehend it? ... And suddenly the memory revealed itself. The taste was that of the little piece of madeleine which on Sunday mornings at Combray (because on those mornings I did not go out before mass), when I went to say good morning to her in her bedroom, my Aunt Léonie used to give me, dipping it first in her own cup of tea or tisane. The sight of the little madeleine had recalled nothing to my mind before I tasted it. And all from my cup of tea.

Lynch was giving both the characters, and the audience, a taste of Laura; but it wasn't enough. The moment Leland kills Maddy is the moment it is revealed to the audience that Leland is the killer. Just prior to brutally attacking Maddy, Leland looks into the mirror and reveals himself as Bob, the entity responsible for the death of Laura. It becomes clear that he is possessed by Bob and in a way Maddy is possessed, too—not by Bob, but by Laura. There is no question that Maddy's physical embodiment of Laura leads to her death.

David Lynch films Leland killing Maddy so that the audience can see Laura murdered. This scene is a reflection of what happened before the series began, a reimagining of the catalyst to the story, of the gruesome moment the audience has been craving to glimpse.

Laura Palmer and her double, Maddy, are also reflections of the doubles in Alfred Hitchcock's *Vertigo*. Lynch, an admitted Hitchcock fan, often uses foils, if not literal doubles, of female characters in his films. In *Vertigo*, the actress Kim Novak played two roles: that of an ethereal blonde, Madeleine Elster (her first name, also a reference to Proust), and that of a down-to-earth brunette, Judy Barton. We see this Hitchcockian influence in the roles of Dorothy Valens and Sandy Williams in *Blue Velvet*, Renee Madison and Alice Wakefield in *Lost Highway*, and, of course, Laura Palmer and Maddy Ferguson in *Twin Peaks*.

It is no coincidence that Maddy's last name is Ferguson, the last name of the protagonist Jimmy Stewart plays in *Vertigo*. Stewart's character dreams of having Madeleine to himself. If he'd been able to marry her, her name would be Madeleine Ferguson; however, such a marriage could never take place, of course, because Madeleine Elster is dead. This doesn't stop Stewart's character from trying, though, as he dresses Judy up to play the role of Madeleine. In the film, Madeleine is not Madeleine, she is playing a role of Madeleine who is playing the role of her deceased grandmother, Carlotta Valdes, who died by suicide. *Vertigo's* plot hinges on the death of a female character that dies before the movie begins, a mechanism that Lynch employs in *Twin Peaks*. Like Stewart's character in *Vertigo*, Agent Cooper is obsessed with bringing the dead person back to life. We see this objective of Cooper's symbolically in the original series, through his investigation of her murder, and literally in *Twin Peaks: The Return*, when he physically travels back in time to save Laura from her death.

It is worth mentioning that this premise is also reflected in the myth of Orpheus, specifically in regard to his compulsive and, frankly, desperate quest to journey to the underworld to rescue his dead wife. Cocteau's *Orpheus* clearly had an influence on both Hitchcock and Lynch.

The characters in *Twin Peaks*, the audience itself, and the director, David Lynch, fell in love with Laura Palmer and that love turned into an obsession. When asked by biographer Chris Rodley why Lynch chose to embark on a prequel to *Twin Peaks*, he stated, "At the end of the series, I felt sad. I couldn't get myself to leave the world of *Twin Peaks*. I was in love with the character of Laura Palmer and her contradictions: radiant on the surface but dying inside. I wanted to see her live, move and talk. I was in love with that world and I hadn't finished with it."[9] How could Lynch be finished with it when the network finished the show for him? The character of Laura Palmer had transcended the show and embedded herself in pop culture.

The one thing Lynch valued more than anything in the creative process was artistic freedom, and in the case of movies and television, that means retaining *final cut*—he got to make the decisions involving his stories and the characters in them. He has said that not having final cut on his movie *Dune* caused him to feel suicidal, and there's no question that his insistence for complete creative and budgetary control over *Twin Peaks: The Return* was the result of the network interference he experienced in the first two seasons of the show. After the killer was revealed and the murder of Laura Palmer solved, the viewership of the original

THE TAO OF TWIN PEAKS

series declined and the audience disappeared. The golden goose had been killed, along with its supply of golden eggs. Without Laura Palmer, there was, and is, no *Twin Peaks*.

In an effort worthy of Proust, David Lynch sought to bring the memory of Laura Palmer to life on-screen in *Fire Walk with Me*. This was not because we didn't get to see enough of her in the series; rather, it was because we didn't get to see any of her. What we saw of her in the series was merely a plot-point. Laura Palmer was the seed that grew into the tree of *Twin Peaks*. The tree and its branches were the show's storylines and the characters sprouted from those storylines, but Laura Palmer herself remained underground. This idea was literally manifested in the burial of her body in Season 1. The prequel was an attempt to humanize this plot-point, to place flesh upon the bones of this screenwriting device, and it succeeded. Despite a vitriolic reaction at the Cannes Film Festival and scathing reviews by numerous critics, *Fire Walk with Me* is a searing, uncompromising and truthful portrait of a young woman struggling to survive a life in which her father rapes and abuses her while her mother does nothing about it. This film is Laura Palmer's subjective experience of growing up under such conditions and it provides the lens through which the audience views her reality: that of an incest survivor whose reality is distorted. Lynch's artistic styles of surrealism and expressionism offer the perfect palette from which to paint this painful portrait.

As he approached the making of this film, Lynch knew it must end with the death of his beloved character; the character he was now bringing back to life on the screen, however briefly. The working title of the film included the subtitle, *The Last Seven Days of Laura Palmer*. The irony of bringing Laura back to life on-screen is that Lynch is bringing her back to the worst days of her life: the week she sees through the illusion of Bob and identifies her father as her rapist and that rapist kills her. It's a kind of torture for the character. While some accused Lynch of being a sadist, I believe he was the furthest thing from it. What was his ultimate endgame in staging such a thing?

It all comes back to his theme: the restoration of balance, and in this case, the balance between the good and the bad.

In the television series, Lynch explored what abuse looks like. Laura Palmer was dead, and all he could allow the viewer to do was glimpse her life from the outside, like the other characters on the show. It was an outside-looking-in approach. In the film, however, he explored what abuse feels like. He placed the film inside Laura Palmer's first-person point of view. It was an inside-looking-out approach. He had to explore the subject matter from both sides.

In her essay from the anthology, *Full of Secrets: Critical Approaches to Twin Peaks*, Diane Stevenson writes about the split between Leland and Bob and the two sides of Laura Palmer: "Victims of abuse may not only split themselves into different personalities as a defense mechanism but they may split the abuser in like manner—commonly into a good and a bad figure."[10]

Some of Laura Palmer's secrets came out in the series, secrets like drug use, prostitution, and her incestuous relationship with her father. However, perhaps because the characters and audience couldn't witness such hidden traits and traumas, and she was presented as a victim of circumstance, Laura Palmer rose above it all. Laura was always an idea in the series, not a character. She was a venerated, if not saintly, figure; the lives of the characters revolved around her. In other words, she wasn't human; she was superhuman.

The character of Laura Palmer, her state of being, was out of balance. *Fire Walk with Me* rectifies this, eliminating the humor and lightheartedness present in the series and confronting head-on the horrors of Laura's abuse and its destructive results. This brings us back to the image of the yin and yang. It's the Tao of *Twin Peaks*: in order to examine and consequently appreciate the good, we must also examine and, to an extent, understand the bad before we are able to go back and live in the light on the side of the good. One side cannot exist without the other, therefore neither side can be ignored. While Maddy served as a proxy Laura, she was not the other side of her. She was not the opposite because Laura was not just one thing.

Laura is one of Lynch's characters who embodies two characters within herself, unlike the characters that he splits into two separate characters. It can be argued that Dorothy Valens and Sandy Williams in *Blue Velvet* are, figuratively speaking, two sides of the same person, the person whom Jeffrey, played by

Kyle MacLachlan, is in love with. He's not in love with one of them; rather, he's in love with both of them. He is attracted to both the corrupted and the uncorrupted. Lynch makes these types of character assignments even more clear in *Lost Highway*, when he directs the same actress, Patricia Arquette, to play two different characters who are essentially the two sides of the same person: the real one and the one imagined by her husband.

There are some people, particularly critics, who find *Fire Walk with Me* to be one of David Lynch's more difficult films. I agree it's one of his more difficult films to experience, emotionally, but not necessarily to understand. While the series remains the foundation for the film, and its symbols are present, the film is as realistic in its subjectivity as it can possibly be. The prologue to the film, which stands on its own, suggests there will be symbols that will need to be decoded throughout the remainder of the film. However, these symbols are not meant for the audience, but rather for Laura Palmer. Through the use of dramatic irony, we are fully aware going into the film that Leland Palmer is Laura's abuser and she will die at his hands. But Laura doesn't know this. Perhaps audiences were taken aback by the prequel because there were no investigations for us to undertake. In fact, Agent Cooper is barely even in the movie, and he's not investigating anything outside the disappearance of Agent Chet Desmond, a character that was created as a substitute for Cooper since Kyle MacLachlan declined to play a large role in the film.

Our hearts break for Laura Palmer as we watch her discover and come to grips with what we've already discovered and have been coming to grips with over the course of watching the series. It is a brutal experience, but an artistically profound one. We are presented with a woman split in half, but not through metaphor, through genuine human experience. Through his trademark surrealistic and expressionistic style, Lynch makes us experience the abuse and its effects as she experiences them. He makes us stand witness to the crimes and corruption of this person's life; it hopefully sparks anger inside us, anger at a society that can turn a blind eye to such things in the name of being taboo or considered hard to look at. Lynch said, "The home is a place where things can go wrong," and most of his work explores this idea, particularly *Twin Peaks*.[11] At Laura Palmer's graveside funeral in the series, Laura's ex-boyfriend, Bobby Briggs, bursts out yelling: "Everybody knew she was in trouble, but we didn't do anything. You want to know who killed Laura? You did. We all did." Perhaps this speaks to the collective denial—both the characters' and ours—of what was happening, specifically the incest and murder of a young girl at the hands of her father, who for all intents and purposes, is a pillar of his community. This critique is at it harshest when we consider Sarah Palmer's denial and her selective memory, which sought to ignore what was happening under her nose. We, as a society, did kill Laura Palmer; we don't want to confront such abhorrence, so we choose not to. It is the desire to maintain those freshly painted white picket fences by keeping the darkness corralled within them that has led to more harm inside, and outside, of the home. The act of containing such darkness, confining it within the walls, itself is incestuous; not letting the light of the world into the closed off domain of the house. It is the house as a prison and its white picket fence as the bars.

The moment of clarity Bobby provides doesn't last, as his rivalry with James Hurley cuts it off short. Any semblance of the thought resonating within those in attendance is further destroyed when a distraught Leland Palmer jumps onto Laura's coffin as it is being lowered into the ground. This is a moment of extreme inappropriateness, which is funny in its absurdity, as the lowering mechanism malfunctions causing the coffin to jerk up and down while Leland grasps onto it. Yet, even though its farcical nature is emphasized again in the following scene, when Shelly reenacts it with a napkin holder for laughing customers at the diner, it becomes a very different scene if the farce is stripped away.

The funeral scene cuts between the grave's edge on which Sarah kneels, chastising Leland and yelling at him to not "ruin this too," and a medium shot of Leland atop the coffin, weeping while he embraces the wooden shell of his dead daughter as they move up and down together. Armed with the knowledge of who killed Laura, we could read this moment as an allusion to the sexual relationship between father and daughter and a foreshadowing of what we will learn. Laura is shielded from her father by the coffin, a ghastly circumstance she ultimately chose, just as she safeguarded herself from him raping her by disassociating both her personality and her father's physical identity. Similar to the way Ed Sullivan's camera operators filmed Elvis, Leland is framed from the waist up; and just as with Elvis and his pelvis, the absence of *what's below* only brings our attention to *what's below*.

The allusion also includes the mother, who sits at the edge of the abyss, staring down into it but not stopping what is happening. It is also evident that, while emotionally affected, Sarah cares more about how this scene looks to other people; in other words, people outside of the house, not inside. Maintaining the appearance of that perfect white picket fence is the priority. "Don't ruin this too!" What does the "too" refer to here? It seems to me that the answer is clear. Leland ruined Laura, and Sarah let it happen.

In the film, Lynch tears the farce off like a band-aid over a cut that just won't stop bleeding. He balances the absence of Laura in the series with the presence of her in the film, and that presence is a downward spiral. He presents us with the ruin that is Laura Palmer; however, that ruin isn't without hope.

In his essay for *Wrapped In Plastic* magazine entitled "The Realization of Laura Palmer," John Thorne incisively notes that the ending of *Fire Walk with Me* is not the same ending as it was written in the screenplay. The following is an excerpt from the script:

```
INT. TRAIN CAR — NIGHT

Leland hoists Laura up so that she hovers facing
the floor a foot off the ground. He places a mirror
on the floor directly under her face.

IN THE MIRROR

Laura sees herself turn into Bob.

Leland screams into space.

                    LELAND
          DON'T MAKE ME DO IT.

                    LAURA
          NO, YOU HAVE TO KILL ME.

                    LELAND
          I always thought you knew it was me.

                    LAURA
          (into Bob in the mirror)
          NO! YOU CAN'T HAVE ME.
               (to Leland)
          KILL ME.
```

```
EXT. TRAIN CAR — NIGHT

Gerard arrives outside. He bangs on the train
door.

                    GERARD
          LET ME IN. LET ME IN.

The door opens a little bit because Ronette is
pushing it with her feet. Gerard reaches up to
help her when suddenly she flies over his head
having been hit.

Ronette hits the ground, her unconscious head bent
back at an odd angle.

ECU: GERARD

He listens to the sounds of murder inside the
train car.

INSIDE THE TRAIN CAR

Laura screaming.

Knife entering flesh.

Bob screaming.

Bloody knife thru the air.

Leland screaming.[12]
```

In the film, while Leland holds Laura and Ronette captive in the train car, an angel appears to Ronette. Laura sees the angel, too, but seems aware it is not there to save her. Seconds later, Ronette's hands become untied. Ronette opens the door, just as she does in the script, and then gets hit and pushed out by Leland. The most glaring omission in this part of the screenplay is that of the owl ring—the gold ring with an owl intaglio carved into a green stone. This is the same ring that Teresa Banks wore before Leland murdered her. It appeared to Laura earlier in a dream, in which Agent Cooper warned her not to take it. The ring is also directly connected to the entities that inhabit the Red Room, as we see the Arm holding it and referring to it as a wedding ring of sorts earlier in the film. Phillip Gerard, aka Mike, throws the ring into the train car after Ronette falls out of it to the ground. Leland closes the door and Laura puts on the ring. It is this action that serves as the catalyst for her murder.

It seems clear that Bob wants to possess Laura, not kill her, but when she puts the ring on her finger, Bob is compelled to kill her. It's as though the ring is the trigger of a gun that fires Bob as its bullet. While the ring can doom the person wearing it, according to co-writer Robert Engels, it can also "empower" the wearer.[13] This moment is critical and changes the reading of the end of the film, yet the idea was not conceived in the writing stage. This idea, along with the motif of angels—both visually and in the dialogue—were added later, most likely during the shooting process.

Thorne argues that Palmer's death was submissive in the script, but Lynch added the ring, which she puts on herself, in order to transform her into a more proactive character. Thorne writes: "In *Fire Walk with Me*, Lynch committed to bringing Laura to life, but had to follow her story to its pre-defined end—the one in which Laura is killed. How could he make her an active character in this scenario? How could she grow and change and take action?"[14] In the series, Dr. Jacoby suggests that Laura *wanted* to die and, in a sense, let the murder happen to her. The screenplay for the film appears to echo this notion.

While both outcomes in the screenplay and the finished film result in Laura's death, Thorne suggests that by usurping control of the ring and using its power, she actively resists Bob and chooses good over evil.

I agree to an extent; however, I don't believe this makes her quite active enough if the intention is to emphasize her choice of good over evil. If she doesn't put on the ring, and is thus unable to resist Bob, that does not mean she chooses evil over good. Evil triumphs, but she doesn't choose for it to triumph. Supplementing angels in the storyline provides an additional layer of meaning and lends insight to the revised ending. Laura is not choosing good over evil; she is choosing to be good in its ongoing battle with evil. Choice of one thing over another implies imbalance. However, the choice to be one thing in order to correct the other implies balance. In other words, evil cannot be eliminated, but it can be counterbalanced. Earlier in the film, when Donna asks Laura the question, if she were falling in space, would she slow down or move faster and faster, Laura replies, "Faster and faster. And for a long time, you wouldn't feel anything. Then you would burst into fire. Forever. And the angels wouldn't help you. Because they've all gone away."

Laura's description of herself in space is reminiscent of stars burning in the night sky—the larger the star, the faster it burns hydrogen and the brighter and hotter it becomes. She does not realize she has become a star, energy created by fusion, rather than the opposite, a nuclear bomb caused by division. Her ultimate purpose is not to be the victim, but rather to be the angel to Bob's devil. This dichotomy between these characters is made even clearer in Episode 8 of Season 3 when we are presented with both Bob and Laura's origin stories. Laura was created to counterbalance Bob: there cannot be one without the other.

David Lynch was a proponent of ideas in the air, certain zeitgeists that foster creativity, and if we're to consider his practice of Transcendental Meditation and belief in the unified field and interconnectivity of human beings, it is interesting to consider the biggest hit song his art school roommate's band had in the early '80s:

> *Years go by I'm lookin' through a girly magazine*
> *And there's my homeroom angel on the pages in-between.*

Peter Wolf was Lynch's roommate and singer for the J. Geils band and their song, "Centerfold," perfectly encapsulates Laura Palmer. The song explores the question of whether a woman who lives a double life—the innocent schoolgirl and the wild child—is complete. This is what *Twin Peaks* also asks with respect to the character around which the series revolves. For Lynch, she is complete. She can be the angel who is also the centerfold; however, he won't let the centerfold be what she is remembered as. What she will be remembered as is Laura Palmer: the angel.

As she takes her place in the Red Room at the end of *Fire Walk with Me*, and watches television—assumably the show that she started—she realizes that she isn't human. She is more than human. She realizes she is a plot-point, a representation of something much larger, something beyond the scope of the human condition. Through her death, an entire universe came into being and that universe is *Twin Peaks*. She is indeed a star. Laura Palmer is a star; she is known worldwide and the public's desire to find her killer was so powerful it ended up killing the show that she started and then bringing it back 25 years later. She has achieved a type of immortality.

Imagine Laura Palmer watching the opening few minutes of the pilot to *Twin Peaks* in the Red Room and seeing herself be discovered by Pete Martel on the shore, wrapped in plastic, the very beginning of it all. David Lynch resurrected her in *Fire Walk with Me* and he did it again in *Twin Peaks: The Return*. She was not meant for earth, she was meant for the beyond, to restore balance to the Red Room inside of the television. Since her death, she has become an indispensable part of the Red Room—she is the Arm's cousin; she is a fixture there, just as the Arm, Mike, the Giant, and Bob are.

These circumstances are reminiscent of the story of Christ and other universal myths about gods and resurrection. In the case of Christ, he was purported to be the son of God who was sent to earth to die for humanity's sins. While on earth, he was mortal, and as a mortal, he doubted his own angels and supernatural connection to the beyond, unable to communicate with his God while on the cross. "My God, why have you forsaken me?" After dying in one of the most brutal of ways, he was resurrected, as Laura was by Lynch in *Fire Walk with Me*. Jesus stated, "I am the resurrection and the life," which essentially pardons him from death—in other words, death has no hold over him. Neither does it have a hold over Laura Palmer. Laura Palmer's corpse is the life of the show.

Through death she lives, and her reaction of bliss at the end of the film confirms this understanding. She cries tears of relief and joy, and occasionally laughs directly from the gut, as though this is some kind of cosmic joke. The connection to the resurrection of Christ is credible. Look no further than to the ersatz resurrection of Laura Palmer through Maddy Ferguson, disguised as her deceased cousin, in Episode 8 of Season 1, when she appears to Dr. Jacoby. She is standing, having risen from the dead, in Easter Park. Lynch's parents were devout Presbyterians, which is a Christian denomination rooted in the Calvinist tradition. Lynch's brother, John, has said their religion "was an important part of our upbringing."[15] Their days in Sunday school studying the teachings of Jesus Christ impacted the young men, and for David, what he learned might have contributed to his artistic approach in *Fire Walk with Me*. Ray Wise, who played the character of Leland Palmer in both the series and the film, has said that "the last twenty minutes of the film are almost like a religious experience."[16] This experience, I believe, is very much intentional on the part of Lynch.

In the train car sequence, an angel frees a captive Ronette from her bindings. If we examine the narrative logic in this scene and consider reality and its implications, the only person who could have physically freed Ronette was Laura, as it was just her, her father, and Ronette who were present. Ronette could have freed herself, but perhaps Laura freed her, or at least diverted her father's attention so Ronette could escape. Either way, Laura likely saved someone's life by surrendering her own, which contributes to her metaphorical representation later as a supernatural force.

As she stares into the flickering light of the television set in the film's final scene, with Agent Cooper by her side, Laura realizes that she sacrificed herself for *Twin Peaks*. The characters on the show would not exist without her death, and neither would the fans of the show, the people watching the characters and witnessing their lives play out on-screen.

The translucent angel that hovers above her is not so much a separate character, but rather a symbol of what she has become. Laura Palmer is now a goddess among the gods, watching over the characters of *Twin Peaks* on the television inside the Red [Living] Room. She is a modern-day angel and Lynch is her televangelist.

Several years ago, I was fortunate enough to acquire a work of art from Sheryl Lee's personal collection. It is a painting that David Lynch made specifically for Sheryl during the time period between *Twin Peaks*, the original series, and *Fire Walk with Me*. The piece is entitled *Pheng* and it depicts a naked female figure with angelic wings rising from the ground and hovering in the air. The ground is part of a desolate and barren landscape, a single palm tree the only sign of life amidst it. The palette is black and grey and Lynch used a variety of methods to depict the imagery, including burning the paper and carving into it with a knife. It's as though the angelic image was born of fire and a sharpened blade. A thought bubble protrudes from the figure's mouth, inside of which is the word "Pheng."

According to Chinese mythology, a peng is a giant bird that

evolved from a fish, the name of which is a variant of the Chinese character "feng." Feng is often associated with *fenghuang*, the term for the Chinese phoenix. The Buddhist monk Zhi Dun compared the peng's flight to the highest state that a *zhiren* can achieve—*zhiren* is defined as a perfect person, sage or saint. The Chinese phoenix is an immortal bird that represents the element of fire. It is a symbol of harmony and balance between yin and yang. It is also considered the start of a new beginning.

Lynch, David. *Pheng*. Mixed media on paper. Courtesy of the author

This painting's connection to Laura Palmer—specifically David Lynch's interpretation of Laura Palmer—seems clear. Lynch provides Laura with a new beginning in *Fire Walk with Me*, as she transforms from sinner to saint, as a means of restoring balance to the *Twin Peaks* universe. Sheryl Lee brings this dead character back to life in the film—a character that Lynch never intended to be alive on-screen—and this painting reflects that idea. Laura Palmer as the phoenix embodies the element of fire. Laura walks with fire, just as the title of the film asserts. She has not been created to put out the fire, but rather to keep the fire under control. In other words, Lynch's metaphorical fire in *Twin*

Peaks will always be burning, but her character was created *from it* in order to bring balance *to it*.

Through her death, Laura transforms from an imperfect human being to a mythological figure. Just as the peng accrued mythological status in ancient Chinese lore, so too has Laura Palmer achieved such status in American pop culture.

WILLIAM DICKERSON

I'M NOT GONNA TALK ABOUT JUDY

Basic Reading Program's Guidance in Reading Series published a book that worked its way through school curriculums across the country from the late '30s through the early '60s. The book is entitled *Bob and Judy* and it depicts little boys and girls going about their everyday activities, its purpose to help children learn to read. On the surface, it's pure '50s idealism; its pages filled with archetypes of classic Americana, archetypes David Lynch explores, and splits in two, in his films. There are rabbits, glasses of milk and a majestic white horse called the Silver King.

This book was in circulation around the time Lynch was in elementary school. Perhaps he read it; perhaps he didn't. Perhaps it was just another example of white picket fence perfection that America was selling at the time, a piece of ephemera to pile on top of the rest, parochial preparation for becoming a civilized human being. In my research, I stumbled upon this book, drawn to the title, of course. I bought a used copy, a first edition from 1936. It's in readable condition, but the pages have decayed and stains mar the illustrations.

Idealized Americana printed upon decomposing paper. This is the very definition of *Lynchian*.

There's no concrete evidence that Lynch came across a copy of this book, or used it as inspiration, but I wanted to start this chapter with this book in mind, as it is precisely the world Lynch seeks to subvert in his oeuvre. While its illustrations may appear superficial, the stains from the hands of readers—perhaps the hands of parents who read it to their children—imbue them with meaning. The incredible responsibility of parents in shaping the lives of their children is at the forefront of *Twin Peaks*. In much of Lynch's work, innocence is represented through teenagers, or young adults, and the corruption of that innocence is sparked by outside forces of nature. These outside forces of nature often originate from inside the home; incest being one example of this type of corruption. In *Twin Peaks*, parents represent both the creators of their child and the destroyers of their child. This dichotomy is perhaps the most striking of Lynchian dichotomies, as its dualism is at once both obvious and remarkably nuanced.

Child sexual abuse is one of the most insidious of abuses. This kind of abuse, this form of rape, is a betrayal of the natural, civilized order and an abdication of parental responsibility. Parents, and members of the parents' generation, are meant to be the protectors of children; the irony being, that in the case of incest, they are also the perpetrators, the types of people they are supposed to be protecting their children from.

As difficult as it may be to understand, Laura Palmer is, at times, portrayed as liking the abuse she endures. This is most evident in her diary entries and audiotapes to Dr. Jacoby. In Laura's last tape to Dr. Jacoby, from Episode 8 of Season 1, she says: "Hey, you remember that mystery man I told you about? Well, if I tell you his name, you're going to be in trouble. He wouldn't be such a mystery man anymore, but you might be history, man. I think, a couple of times, he's tried to kill me. But guess what, as you know, I sure got off on it. Isn't sex weird? This guy can really light my F-I-R-E." She finishes up the message right before her mom enters with "milk and cookies."

The title of the book that inspires this chapter isn't Bob *or* Judy; it's Bob *and* Judy. The title implies that two make a whole; it implies a symbiotic relationship between two people and offers the shared experience between them. Laura Palmer is a single individual, and as the Log Lady puts it in one of her television introductions to the show, "[*Twin Peaks*] is a story of many, but begins with one—and I knew her. The one leading to the many is Laura Palmer. Laura is the one." However, while the story begins with Laura, the one, she cannot exist without two: her parents. Life is created through the intercourse of two, and in *Twin Peaks*, life is also destroyed by two.

If the central question in the original series was "who killed Laura Palmer," the central question in Season 3 is "who is Judy"? There is an answer to both questions. The answers are different, but in a way, the same.

In Mark Frost's book, *Twin Peaks: The Final Dossier*, which continues the story of *Twin Peaks*, Lynch's co-creator makes it clear that the young girl from 1956 in Episode 8 of Season 3 is Sarah Palmer: Sarah Judith Novack Palmer.[17] The inclusion of Sarah's middle name, which was never disclosed throughout the entire series of *Twin Peaks*, or the prequel film, is noteworthy, particularly considering this book was released after Season 3, after the narrative posed the ultimate question: Who is Judy?

According to *The Final Dossier*, Sarah's father was a Defense Department employee who worked in "some small but unspecified subcontractor role on the Manhattan Project."[18] This is an important detail, as it aligns with Lynch's metaphor of evil. If the nuclear bomb is the "evil that men do," then employees like Sarah's father are the evil we let men get away with. There is the crime and then there is the accessory to the crime, and both are bad, perhaps one worse than the other. While Albert Einstein was someone who encouraged President Franklin Roosevelt to develop nuclear weapons, he along with numerous other scientists expressed regret over having worked on the Manhattan Project and helping facilitate such devastation in the Japanese cities of Hiroshima and Nagasaki. It was said about Nazi Germany during World War II, the world woke up to the awareness that one third of the country was killing another one third while the other third watched. This is the insidious balance that is inherent within the concept of evil. If the one third who watched stepped up and did something, the one third doing the killing would, theoretically, be unable to kill the remaining third. They would be outnumbered. For evil to exist, there must be enough people willing to ignore it, and it might be argued that ignoring such acts of evil is worse than the evil itself.

The people who perpetrate evil and the people who ignore it are bedfellows, engaged in an intercourse of malfeasance. This is the intercourse that Bob and Judy are engaged in.

The fact that Mark Frost provides his readers with this background information on Sarah's father implies there is a direct connection to his daughter. It cements our understanding that the little girl in Episode 8 is Sarah Palmer, while also shedding light on some of her character. Just as her father helped facilitate the atomic bomb killing hundreds of thousands of people, she helped facilitate her husband in his sexual abuse and murder of their daughter. Inside the Palmer home resides an unholy trinity of the one who killed, the one who died, and the one who watched.

In the pilot episode of the series, Sarah is the first person to identify the suspect in Laura's murder. In a session with a sketch artist, she depicts the longhaired and bearded man we later learn is called Bob. While we can argue that her vision of Bob is her disassociating from the reality that the perpetrator is Leland, just as Laura disassociates from this fact, a more cynical reading might conclude that she is blaming someone else, and in doing so, sending the authorities off the track of her husband.

The act of blaming another person, event, or circumstance for the troubles one had a part in bringing upon him or herself, is a classic indication of denial. Some denial is more conscious than others; some denial is more innocent than others; some denial is more malevolent than others. I posit that the more involved the employees of the Manhattan Project were, the more they were emotionally affected by its outcome; therefore, it stands to reason that the more Sarah Palmer was involved in facilitating the abuse of their daughter, the more she was emotionally affected by its outcome. As we see in the original series, and more prominently in Season 3, Sarah is crippled with guilt, anger, and confusion; the darkness is perfectly in control of her—she has surrendered control over to the darkness completely. In Season 3, when Sarah removes her face, she reveals the darkness within her. Whereas, when Laura removes her face, she reveals the opposite: brightness. Lynch establishes this interior contrast and makes it specific to these two people, mother and daughter.

Sarah, along with Cooper, and subsequently the audience, is haunted by recurring images of the ceiling fan outside of Laura's bedroom throughout the series. The fan's motor is used by Leland as white noise to cover up the sounds of his sexual liaisons with Laura. While he may have initially believed it provided enough of an audio barrier between his illicit behavior and his wife in his bedroom, Sarah can only be haunted by this image if she knows what it means.

She knows what it means and chooses to listen to the sound of the fan over the sounds of her husband with their daughter. The fan is, thus, a symbol of her denial.

The fan appears again in Season 3 when Deputy Hawk visits Sarah after an incident at a supermarket to check on her well-being. As Hawk arrives at her door, we see a close-up of the fan. Hawk then hears some noise inside, the sounds of someone or something else in the house. This sound is clear to Hawk, and to the audience, but Sarah pays no attention to it. She is ignoring it, just as she ignored the sounds from Laura's bedroom many years ago. The fan is on, once again, drowning out the sounds in the other room.

Another recurring image is the white horse, which appears to Sarah moments before Leland abuses Laura the night before he kills her. Leland drugs her milk to inebriate her during this assault and, presumably, during previous assaults that he perpetrated against their daughter. The white horse is a loaded image and is used as a symbol in numerous cultures, religions, and stories. In the New Testament, the first horseman of the apocalypse rides a white horse, which some scholars interpret to symbolize Christ or the Antichrist. It is notable that the fourth horseman, Death, rides a pale horse as well. In Hinduism, the white horse is emblematic of the sun, an image that seems closely associated with Laura Palmer in Season 3. In Native American mythology, the god Aisoyimstan, who rides a white horse, is the bringer of snow that freezes the earth. It is interesting to consider this characteristic in opposition to the use of fire in *Twin Peaks* and the seeming inability to extinguish it, specifically in regard to the character of Laura Palmer. There is also the white horse Silver

King that is written about and illustrated in the pages of the book *Bob and Judy*.

There may be a firmer connection to the white horse of Greek mythology, a mythology that is referenced throughout *Twin Peaks*. The white horse of Greek lore is Pegasus, a winged horse that was created when Perseus cut off Medusa's head. Pegasus was born from this act of blood. But he was also born of rape. Medusa was once beautiful and pure, until she was raped and impregnated by Poseidon, the god of the sea, in Athena's temple. Athena then punished Medusa for befouling her sacred space by transforming her into a monster that would turn anyone who gazed upon her into stone. Pegasus was the progeny of Medusa and Poseidon, having entered this world through her death.

The white horse as product of rape is a characteristic that is shared with the white horse in Sarah's vision, as the white horse appears when Leland is raping, or preparing to rape, Laura. The exception to this motif is when the horse appears to Sarah just prior to Leland murdering Maddy. He does not rape her, but there is a sexual undertone to his actions, and the parallel to his abuse and murder of Laura is apparent. As the Log Lady mentions in another of her introductions to the show, "Woe to the ones who behold a pale horse." If this line is directed to Sarah, then perhaps her vision is an admission of her guilt; she is aware of what is happening and does nothing to stop it.

After Perseus slays Medusa, he uses her disembodied head to ward off enemies and ultimately bestows it to Athena to place on her shield. This led the ancient Greeks to use the image of Medusa on their shields and on amulets they wore around their necks. These symbolic amulets were referred to as Gorgoneions and purported to divert evil, specifically the evil eye, from the wearer. Their power came from apotropaic magic. *Apotropaic* comes from the Greek word apotrope, which literally means "to turn away." The concept of damage being inflicted through the eyes was solidified through the myth of Medusa, which in turn sparked the idea that evil should not be looked at through the eyes, as it may bring harm to the viewer. Therefore, one must divert the eyes to avoid harm to oneself.

Lynch, however, opposed the idea that evil shouldn't be looked at directly. His work strongly expresses the notion that one must look at and recognize evil in order to be good, to achieve good and be capable of goodness. Simply stated, good people don't divert their eyes from evil; they confront it. In the case of Medusa, she is the victim of rape; however, she is mythologized as a monster, as a fixture of evil. This seems reminiscent of modern society's knee-jerk reactions to uncomfortable topics or taboos, such as rape, child abuse, and incest. It's difficult to look at it all in the eye, so we turn away. The act of turning away, or turning a blind eye to, has been explored in recent analyses of the show, specifically in relation to the Woodsman's dialogue in Episode 8 of Season 3:

The horse is the white of the eyes and dark within.

The mention of the words "horse" and "white" in the same line leads us to make a connection to the motif of the white horse throughout the series. The physical manifestation of the white horse in *Twin Peaks* is unique to Sarah Palmer, as it mostly appears to her—though it also appears later to Agent Cooper in the Red Room—and is tied to her husband's abusive and murderous behavior.

In the intriguing video essay, *Twin Peaks ACTUALLY EX-*

PLAINED (No, Really), by Twin Perfect, the host explores the meaning of the white horse: "What does the white horse mean? When do you see the whites of somebody's eyes? When they are looking the other way. When we see white horses in *Twin*

Peaks, something evil is happening. The white horse represents looking the other way in the face of evil and the darkness we allow into ourselves when we do so."[19] The correlation between the whites of people's eyes and "looking the other way" in the show is a concept that has been advanced online by numerous viewers and bloggers since the airing of Season 3. Therefore, let's explore this further.

Athena, the Greek goddess of wisdom, used Medusa's eyes to ward off evil around her, as she believed evil could not be looked at in the eye, and therefore Medusa's eyes served as a substitute. Athena's spirit animal is the owl, which accompanied her on her shoulder, and due to this association, the owl has become a symbol of wisdom. According to the mythology, the owl revealed truths to her. It counterbalanced her blind side and enabled her to recognize the entire truth of matters at hand. Biologically, the owl's eyes are a significant and powerful attribute, as they are capable of seeing in the dark. In fact, they possess the best night vision of any animal. With respect to pupil dilation, the whiter the owl's eyes, the less light is let in, the less they can see in the darkness. The blacker the owl's eyes, the more light is let in, and the more they can see in the darkness.

The white of their eyes is associated with not seeing; whereas, the black of their eyes is associated with seeing.

While the owl symbolizes wisdom in Greek mythology, the animal has been used by many cultures to symbolize other things, much of which are contradictory. The owl is often portrayed as a protector, as in the case of Athena; however, it has also been known to perpetrate evil. William Wordsworth wrote of the owl as a "bird of doom" at a time when the sounds of owls were associated with the impending deaths of the sick. In ancient Rome, an owl that brought evil upon its people was killed and nailed to the door of the home to which the evil was brought; the idea being the dead owl would counteract the evil it caused and eradicate it from the home. The owl, in this instance, became an apotropaic emblem, similar to the visage of Medusa's head. In both instances, people are not confronting evil directly, as they have installed a buffer, a shield, from such encounters.

The owl is capable of both good and bad, according to the mythologies and traditions of various cultures. In other words, *the owls are not what they seem.*

The owl and its perceived symbolic duality makes it the perfect spirit animal for *Twin Peaks* and also the perfect engraving for the ring Laura uses to protect herself from Bob. Just as the image of the owl has been used throughout history, the ring can be used to either doom or protect the wearer. It can cause, and prevent, death. In *Fire Walk with Me*, despite Agent Cooper's warning to Laura not to take the ring, and our understanding that the ring is associated with evil, Laura takes the ring and places it on her finger at the moment she seeks protection.

Just like the owl itself, the ring is not what it seems. It protects Laura from being possessed by Bob, and in doing so safeguards her soul and leads to immortality through the sacred airwaves of television. The ring is also, clearly, an apotropaic device. It is the equivalent to an amulet adorned with the head of Medusa; for Laura, it protects her against the evil that is hell-bent on possessing her.

Once again, this prop ring reflects David Lynch's overarching theme: we are all capable of good and evil; we must achieve a balance between them, and in order to do that, we must seek to understand both the good and the bad parts of ourselves.

Agent Cooper may not have willingly been "looking the other way" in the Red Room for 25 years while his doppelganger was out perpetrating crimes in the world, but it seems as though he was unaware of Mr. C's activities. If we are to take the two versions of Dale Cooper as a metaphor for the two sides of a single Cooper—i.e., ourselves—then the Cooper trapped inside the Red Room all this time is aware of the evil, but doing nothing about it. The fact that he literally cannot do anything about it may be irrelevant.

In Season 3 Episode 2, the white horse appears to Cooper in the Red Room. Just prior to its appearance, Cooper sits across from, and interacts with, the woman who "feels like she knows" Laura Palmer, played by Sheryl Lee. "But sometimes my arms bend back," she says, playing out the scene in the same fashion as it played out in the first Red Room sequence in Season 1. This scene is, in a sense, a revision of the original scene. It is an audiovisual palimpsest. When Cooper asks her who she is again, she changes her answer to "I am Laura Palmer," as though she is discovering this identity for the first time—it's as though this identity had been repressed up until this moment. She states, "I am dead...yet I live." Like Cooper's hibernation in the Red Room, the character of Laura Palmer has been on stasis the past 25 years. It isn't until David Lynch brings these characters back in *Twin Peaks: The Return* that they're turned on again. Like amnesiacs recovering their memories, Dougie and Carrie Page are recovering their characters, namely Agent Cooper and Laura Palmer. If Cooper had saved Laura from her certain television death, what would she have become over these past 25 years? Carrie Page may be that answer.

After Laura says, "...yet I live," she removes her face to reveal flickering white light into which Cooper stares. The light is reminiscent of the flickering light that Laura stares into at the end of *Fire Walk with Me*, the light of our collective television sets, bringing her character back to life on the screen.

As pointed out in various online forums, when Sheryl Lee was being directed in this Red Room scene, she was referred to on set as Carrie, not Laura, which likely means this character was scripted as Carrie. If she is Carrie at the beginning of the scene, her character arc in this sequence is clear—she recognizes herself as, and thusly becomes, Laura Palmer once again. As the scene plays out, almost exactly the way it did in the original version, Laura approaches Cooper, leans down and kisses him, then whispers something in his ear. In the original scene, we know she whispers "My father killed me." Does she say this to Cooper again? Or has her whisper been revised? If the key question of the original series was "who killed Laura Palmer," and the key question of *Twin Peaks: The Return* is "who is Judy," perhaps it's Judy's identity that Laura whispers in Agent Cooper's ear? If Laura Palmer's original whisper to Agent Cooper in the Red Room was "My father killed me," what could be equally as devastating, or even more disturbing? Perhaps, "My mother knew and did nothing about it."

Immediately following her whisper, Laura's attention is drawn upward as both she and Cooper look above their heads. She screams and begins to deteriorate before being physically pulled up and out of the frame by some supernatural, and perhaps malevolent, force. It is at this moment that the white horse appears to Cooper. Lynch cuts from a medium close-up of Cooper to his direct point of view as a howling wind blows back the red curtains to reveal the horse standing atop the black and white floor in the upper right portion of the frame amidst a void of darkness. The shot cuts back to Cooper's face as he surveys the area with his eyes. As Lynch cuts once again to Cooper's point of view of the horse, the camera begins to track forward, intimating where Cooper's attention is being drawn. When presented with the horse, unlike Sarah Palmer's attention, which focuses directly on the horse, Cooper's attention moves past the horse and continues forward, entering the darkness around it, until the entire frame becomes black. This shot operates as a visual metaphor emphasizing Lynch's theme. Instead of focusing on the white horse, like Sarah, Cooper chooses the opposite of "turning away from" the darkness: he heads straight toward it. And this gives us another interpretation of the line: "The horse is the white of the eyes and dark within."

Lynch may be alluding to General Putnam's purported command to Colonial soldiers at the Battle of Bunker Hill during the Revolutionary War to not "fire till you see the whites of their eyes." Lynch was aware of this famous quotation because he referenced it in his prior work. In a scene in *Blue Velvet*, Dennis Hopper's character Frank Booth can't stand Jeffrey Beaumont looking at him, so he threatens him with the line, "Don't you look at me, fuck. I shoot when I see the whites of the eyes." The defending Colonial soldiers needed to glimpse the whites of the enemy's eyes in order to be close enough to hit them with their bullets. These were also men who wanted to kill them; their eyes reflected a darkness inside that they had to destroy. Unlike Twin Perfect's assessment of the phrase in *Twin Peaks*, the whites of eyes could very well equate to looking toward something, not looking away.

This notion of confronting the enemy eye-to-eye corresponds with Lynch's theme of confronting the darkness—the darkness in front of us and inside of us. We must enter the darkness and open our eyes, and like the owls see it for what it is, in order to achieve balance. We must balance the bright with the dark, or one will outweigh the other; it becomes a swinging pendulum, not a yin and yang. We must strive for the equilibrium of the black and white zigzag floor.

Leland and Sarah Palmer represent both the capacity to

perpetrate evil and the will to ignore, and thus facilitate, such evil. The latter speaks to a more widespread problem and, subsequently, a worse problem due to its pervasiveness. I've spent a lot of time writing and making films about mental illness and I often explore the stigmatization of the subject. People find it quite difficult to talk about mental illness, even though it affects one out of four people in the United States, because the topic has been treated as taboo. The same can be said about domestic violence and sexual abuse; no one wants to think about it happening, but it most certainly is happening, and the blind eyes that are turned away from it are what allow it to continue to happen. I believe that Lynch shines a spotlight on such abuses as a means of bringing them to his viewers' attention. Such abuses go unnoticed, as they're safely committed within those white picket fences, and exposure is inhibited by our collective denial of such unthinkable incidents. We, as a culture, avert our eyes because we don't want to look into the eyes of the forbidden, and that avoidance is our sin. It's the light that ultimately exposes the darkness, and it is David Lynch who is turning it on—he literally shines a spotlight on Maddy while she is being murdered.

In the first two seasons of *Twin Peaks*, Bob was created to emotionally disturb the audience with the evil that men do, unlike most other crime shows at the time, which concerned themselves not with the emotional effects of violence on their characters, but rather with answering the question of "who did it?" Unlike *Twin Peaks*, most television in its era was solely focused on solving the crimes, not examining the consequences of the crimes. However, much of *Twin Peaks*' audience, and the network execs at CBS, wanted the show to conform to the prevailing formula—we wanted to know the identity of the killer, so that's what we got, and then we moved on. *Twin Peaks: The Return* is meant to disturb the audience with the evil that is ignored and what ignoring it leads to. We ignored the evil in the first season. That's what the show, following the first two seasons, is about. It is just as David Bowie's character Phillip Jeffries states in *Fire Walk with Me*, "I'm not gonna talk about Judy; in fact, we're not gonna talk about Judy at all."

Bob is bad, but Judy is worse. Bob is Leland Palmer; Judy is his wife and, collectively, the one third of the populace who watches as another one third kills the other.

WILLIAM DICKERSON

EPISODE 8: THE RAPE OF SARAH PALMER

Episode 8 of Season 3 has already attained legendary status, and that status is not unwarranted, as I consider the episode among David Lynch's finest works. It is unique in its structure, tone, and visual style when compared to the other episodes in the season. There is a reason for that, as it serves as the origin story for the good and evil that exists in the show.

Occurring at approximately the midpoint of the series, this episode seems to eschew the formula of the show—if one can call it a formula. It begins normally enough, as it picks up from where the prior episode left off: Mr. C and Ray have escaped from prison and are driving to an enigmatic location called the Farm. The ride to the Farm is fraught with suspense, as the idea of a mutual double-cross is threaded into the fabric of the scene. Mr. C wants the coordinates Ray has memorized, and as we'll see in a minute or two, Ray wants Mr. C dead, as per the instructions of the elusive Phillip Jeffries.

When Ray shoots Mr. C, both Mr. C and the audience are surprised, as we observe this moment through Mr. C's point of view. This is an important distinction. When we experience Mr.

C's storylines, Lynch solidifies the show's point of view within his perspective. With the exception of *Fire Walk with Me*, it is quite clear that the audience's primary lens through which it views, and ultimately experiences, *Twin Peaks*, is Special Agent Dale Cooper. The audience enters *Twin Peaks* with him in the pilot episode, and while we witness other characters in their own storylines, they are all in one way or another related to Cooper's investigations. The audience is the detective, just as Cooper is. This is the audience's role in most mysteries. Therefore, when the good Dale Cooper gets locked in the Black Lodge and is replaced on the ground with his doppelganger, the malevolent Mr. C, the audience is already primed to see the world from his vantage point. When we are witness to Mr. C's scenes, we mostly experience them through him; when we are witness to Cooper in the lodge, and Cooper in the form of Dougie Jones, we primarily experience these scenes through them.

This dichotomy of points of view is as it should be, since Lynch intentionally wants the audience to emotionally and psychologically experience the show through both the good characters and the bad characters, through their good choices and bad choices, and through the consequences of those choices. This filmmaking choice is perfectly aligned with Lynch's underlying theme of balance. It also throws the audience off-guard at the beginning of Episode 8.

Mr. C's skills in the black arts of evil seem unparalleled; he is the Jason Bourne of badness. He is about to crush Ray like the bug that he is, but then Lynch momentarily brings us into Ray's point of view, filming him from the front as Mr. C points his gun at him from behind. We know Ray has a gun before Mr. C does, because we see him pull it out from his waistband outside the view of Mr. C. We're also emotionally with Ray as we hear Mr. C's trigger click without firing any bullets. After Ray says, "I tricked you...fucker," and shoots Mr. C, Lynch continues using Ray's POV, moving with him as he approaches the prone body of his victim. He leans over, and then the fun begins: we are as shocked as Ray is when translucent Woodsmen—lumberjack-like drifters—scurry from the woods, seemingly out of thin air, and rush to the aid of Mr. C.

We stand in horror, with Ray, as we witness these supernatural entities smear a mixture of dirt and blood over the body and then the head of Mr. C. It's as though they've applied a medieval war paint of his bodily fluids to his face. The superimposed Woodsmen dance in a circle around him, as though participating in a ceremonial raising of the dead. Stroboscopic light flashes onto Ray, who continues to watch; perhaps it's the light of television showcasing its magical ability to bring its characters back to life, as it does so often. An orb-like egg begins to rise from Mr. C's stomach containing the image of Bob, smiling at Ray. Ray, terrified, escapes, hopping into the car and tearing away from the gruesome scene. The scene fades to black, a darkness that is momentarily interrupted by a shot of a half moon. It is a distinct half bright, half dark image, which is quickly consumed by the prevailing darkness of black clouds.

Shortly after this transition, we're back in the Roadhouse as the MC announces the next performer: the Nine Inch Nails. This announcement is an indication that this episode is markedly different than the others. The episodes usually end with a musical performance at the Roadhouse; however, in this episode, we are treated to a performance near its beginning. It's a reversal of the formula up until this point, and an indication that time is about to be reversed, as we begin to enter the past. The song is called "She's Gone Away," and Trent Reznor, the lead singer of Nine Inch Nails and repeated Lynch collaborator, accompanies its heavy, repetitive bass guitar notes with his electrifying singing:

Yeah, I was watching on the day she died...

The lyrics have metafictional significance, as they reference the show inside of the show itself. Reznor appears to refer to the moment he, along with collective TV watchers around the world, watched as Laura Palmer's dead body, wrapped in plastic, washed up on the shore in the pilot episode of *Twin Peaks*. The line also is a reminder of Sarah (Judy), Laura's mother, and the notion of passively standing by and watching while someone is put in danger, abused, or even killed. Television is a passive activity, a form of entertainment that demands attention, but encourages inaction and welcomes anonymity. We get to witness, and even enjoy, criminal and morally corrupt behavior without having to take responsibility and endure concrete consequences.

As mentioned previously, in *Fire Walk with Me*, when Donna asks Laura the question, if she were falling in space, would she slow down or move faster and faster, Laura replies, "Faster and faster" until she "burst into fire" and "the angels wouldn't help" because "they've all gone away." One of Laura's triggers to despair is the idea that her angels have gone away, that they've abandoned her, perhaps due to her own destructive choices and self-perceived wickedness. She is not cognizant, at least perhaps until the end of the film, that she, herself, is the show's angel; that she is just as powerful as Bob and possesses the power to fight and counterbalance evil on her own. The angels that have "gone away" are just a reflection of her own self-doubt.

Nine Inch Nails' performance of the song is powerful, its sonic and lyrical repetitions digging a primordial groove into our brains. The recurring lyric, "she's gone away," is both hyper-specific in its reference to Laura Palmer, and also universally unspecific, and therefore generally relatable to all of those watching and listening. Whether it's through heartbreak or death—both tragedies in themselves—we've all had someone who's gone away, never to return, outside the miracle of home video or broadcast television.

The line, "We keep licking while the skin turns black," may be a reference to acral lick dermatitis, a condition found primarily in dogs that is notable due to its self-perpetuating nature. Dogs, whether in reaction to an itch, stress, or even boredom, repeatedly lick an area of its body until it creates an abrasion. The wound this creates continues to worsen because it prompts further licking, and further licking aggravates the wound. This sometimes culminates with the skin turning black. If we are to view this as an analogy to ourselves, we may perceive this cycle of healing and hurting as similar to the cycle of abuse and how some people are drawn to it—*we keep licking the skin*—while simultaneously refusing to acknowledge, or take responsibility, for it—*until the skin turns black*. Being compelled to watch and witness the abuse—and the effects of the abuse—of Laura Palmer and being unable to acknowledge similar abuses we may be aware of, or even perpetrate, in our own lives is abjectly hypocritical and Lynch wants us to realize that.

This intention is baked into the pilot episode. It's his modus operandi behind the entire series of *Twin Peaks*: he wants us to focus on the consequences of the murder of Laura Palmer, what the tragedy does to an entire town of people, and not focus on the murder itself. The investigation is the itch that needs to be scratched, but if we keep licking that part of ourselves, we will never be satisfied and the wound will never heal. If *Twin Peaks* was meant to adhere to this cycle, it would have become a show that was just like any other crime drama: an episode begins with a murder, and it ends with the solving of that murder; and in the next episode, the cycle repeats again. The problem is, in viewing the drama presented in such a transitory manner, we become more and more disconnected and detached from the lives of the characters and the humanity of the show.

If we were to, as Reznor puts it, "Cut along the length (but you can't get the feeling back)," we will have substituted cookie-cutter formula for genuine human emotion. After the show revealed who killed Laura Palmer, it succumbed to television formula and, in a sense, turned black and died. For Lynch, the show did turn black, the audience having kept licking that same spot, and in Episode 8 of Season 3, it is the blackness of death that manifests itself.

The music of Nine Inch Nails merges with the sound of wind and ambience in the barren landscape as Lynch cuts to where Mr. C's unresponsive body lies. The music transforms into sound design, its feedback swelling in volume just before it abruptly cuts out as Mr. C sits up into frame, his eyes opening wide as he returns to life. The screen then cuts to black before fading into a black and white image of another barren landscape: White Sands, New Mexico, on July 16th, 1945 at 5:29 am.

This is the time and place of the Trinity Nuclear Bomb Test. And that is what Lynch invites his audience to watch, and then enter, from the bomb's point of view. The shot is epic, and necessarily so. It begins on the outskirts of the desert, presumably where the members of the Manhattan Project stood as they witnessed the blast. It starts at a distance, because the onlookers are at a distance; naturally, they must position themselves as far away from the bomb as possible to prevent residual harm. This distance between bomb and onlooker also extends to the audience of the show. Just like we were "watching on the day she [Laura Palmer] died," the scientists in White Sands were watching when standard warfare died and a new threat of apocalyptic proportions was born.

One of these scientists and director of the Los Alamos Laboratory, J. Robert Oppenheimer, remarked about watching this event: "We knew the world would not be the same. A few people laughed, a few people cried. Most people were silent. I remembered the line from the Hindu scripture, the Bhagavad Gita: Vishnu is trying to persuade the Prince that he should do his duty and, to impress him, takes on his multi-armed form and says, 'Now I am become Death, the destroyer of worlds.' I suppose we all thought that, one way or another."[20]

In stark contrast to the perspectives of these scientists, the power of Lynch's camera and imagination do not leave his audience standing on the side; he does not let them off the hook. To do so would be immoral—just like the Judy-esque scientists who were able to maintain their distance, and perhaps later in life, compartmentalize their roles in the experiment. Lynch moves his camera forward, taking us inside the bomb blast itself, inside this harbinger of worldwide death and destruction.

As the bomb explodes and the camera heads toward the blast, Krzysztof Penderecki's "Threnody to the Victims of Hiroshima" begins to shriek in the soundtrack. There is a reason Penderecki dedicated this composition to the victims of the world's first nuclear bomb attack, and that is because the form of the music matches the form of the bomb. Instead of focusing on melody and the harmony between instruments, the composition focuses on the disharmony between its musical elements. It employs the technique of *sonorism*, which focuses on the sonic characteristics of a song, most of which are non-musical, in an effort to create a form free of the bounds of harmony and formulaic composition. It is a configuration that centers on counterpoint rather than synchronization.

The effect of listening to these sounds is counterintuitive, just as it's counterintuitive to push into a nuclear explosion, rather than back away from it. As we meet the mushroom cloud and enter the smoke, we are met with an avant-garde short film, using techniques similar to those developed by experimental filmmaker Stan Brakhage. Lynch's film-within-a-film operates in the same manner as the music: it breaks down the formula of composition into its basic elements. It focuses on visual characteristics; the elements that make up images, not the images themselves.

Brakhage created his films by physically manipulating the

film stock, rather than using a camera. He would scratch, tape, and paint individual frames for a unique effect. On one hand, this gave him complete control over every literal frame; on the other, when run through a projector, the film took on a completely different life, a life completely out of his control. It is almost impossible to predict what the whole film will look like when the artistic focus is spent on single frames. It's akin to imagining what an entire forest looks like by looking solely at one tree at a time. It also has another effect; this process brings what is still and lifeless into motion through 24 frames per second of life.

Brakhage's films seek to expose the granular, the particulates that go unseen by the naked eye, the bits and pieces that make up the substance of a cinematic frame. Lynch exposes the subatomic particles at the core of this explosion in a similar manner, manipulating black and white shapes in an effort to highlight the chaos that is being unleashed. He magnifies the experience of nuclear fission, reaching beyond the lens of his camera to the chemical reactions within—a neutron bombards and splits the nucleus of an atom, releasing neutrons that scatter and collide with more atoms, splitting them, which release more neutrons, creating a chain reaction that discharges an enormous amount of energy.

The concept of birth and death is embedded into nuclear power: it can both create and destroy, at levels that extend far beyond the grasp of man, and there must be a balance between these two disparate functions, in order to control the chaos at the core of such power. However, the very concept of exercising control with respect to a nuclear bomb is an act of hubris. And, for Lynch, it is through such hubris that evil is generated.

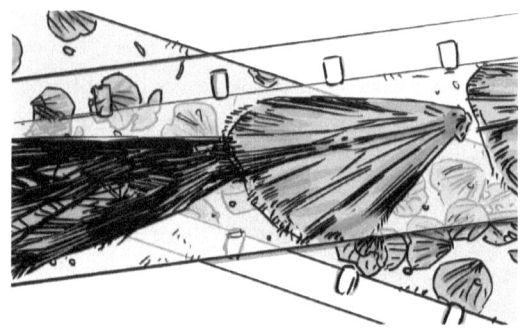

This sequence in Episode 8 of *Twin Peaks: The Return* is perhaps most reminiscent of Brakhage's film *Mothlight*, in which Brakhage compressed the wings of dead moths, blades of grass and flower petals between two pieces of 16mm splicing tape and fashioned them into a film print, sending the light of a projector through the translucent shapes and connecting them all together in a moving collage of images.

The similarity to this film is notable not just because of its innovative process, but also because of its evocation of life and death. Brakhage was prompted to make this film when he came across dead moths that had been drawn to the luminance of light bulbs, an attraction that ultimately killed them. The technique was a resurrection of sorts. While the light was what killed them, he used it to bring them back to life; that is, through the light of a film projector. Like the opposing results of a nuclear reaction, the light both kills and creates, and he sought to present this dichotomy in his film.

The end results of both *Mothlight* and this Episode 8 sequence look quite similar, specifically, in their sharp juxtapositions of black and white lines, shapes, and tones. They are both, simultaneously, formed and formless. Lynch's sequence speaks to the chaos at the subatomic level of a nuclear reaction. On a symbolic, perhaps even Jungian, level, familiar forms take shape: rapidly moving shapes that are sperm-like in appearance scatter haphazardly around the frame. These images not only bring to mind the microscopic images of the female egg being bombarded by spermatozoa, which is not unlike the nuclear bombardment of an atom, but also conjure recollections of the sperm motifs in Lynch's *Eraserhead*. There is no question that the audience is witnessing the birth of something here, and for Lynch, it is the birth of manmade evil—the audience is witnessing man's modern original sin.

Lynch then cuts to a depiction of fire, the camera hurtling toward it, and then to a series of explosions, presumably part of the bomb's nuclear chain reaction. The explosions range in color and texture; while terrifying, no doubt, Lynch depicts them with a kind of beauty. There is a sense of awe and wonder that envelops us as we watch the bomb from within the bomb. Similar to the famous Stargate Sequence in the final moments of Stanley Kubrick's, *2001: A Space Odyssey*, we are transfixed by the quasi-psychedelic journey into something off-limits to the senses of man.

This space-like departure in imagery is disrupted as the sequence fades into the scene at the Convenience Store. The chaos of the subatomic particles and chain reaction explosions are replaced by the chaos of stop-motion Woodsmen moving forwards and backwards in time as they enter and exit the store. The *mise en scène* oscillates between light and dark, clear air and smoke, flashes and shadows, mimicking the sights and staccato sounds of the inside of the nuclear explosion. The particles have become people, scattering into, and ultimately infecting, the surroundings—surroundings that are ubiquitous, universal, as commonplace and collectively recognizable as your local convenience store. There is also a distinct aspect of evil that embraces convenience; it is a whole lot more convenient to use one plane to drop one bomb that kills millions of people, rather than killing them individually and having to look them in the eyes while doing so.

Just as the camerawork becomes more chaotic and unhinged with respect to lens focus and movement, Lynch cuts to a black void and a bulbous entity called "Experiment" floating through it. This entity regurgitates a series of eggs, held together by a viscous substance, the largest of which holds the image of Bob within it. This is the mythological birth of Bob in the universe that is *Twin Peaks*. This is his origin story. His creation is immediately followed by an eruption of fire so abrupt and intense it feels like it threatens to incinerate the fabric of this universe. The music emphasizes this harshness, underscoring it with sonic screeching.

Then there is a moment of respite: an unformed gobbet of gold gliding toward us. The score grows more and more silent as the gold engulfs the camera. This respite is short-lived, though, as shortly thereafter, the discordant strings of "Threnody to the Victims of Hiroshima" kick back in, accompanying the camera as it travels through the bloodstream of this event, passing an onslaught of red platelets. The bomb has gone from being a product of man to becoming man himself. We cannot separate ourselves from the evil we perpetrate—evil is a part of us, just as good is a part of us. For Lynch, this is a biological fact. It is also a biological fact, for Lynch that is, that underneath the blood stream—the corporeal existence of the human being—lies a sea of pure consciousness that is universal and that connects us all to each other. This sea of consciousness is the baseline for all human beings, all of which have the potential for good and evil. It starts at this level, a level that we must cultivate daily in order to achieve the necessary balance in our lives. Lynch cultivated this underlying consciousness by practicing Transcendental Meditation, and his public outspokenness of his practice—he established the David Lynch Foundation to support the teaching of TM—provides us with insight into his art. I am also a practitioner of TM and have often noticed that within the organization, images of "pure consciousness" are portrayed as a purple ocean, not unlike the purple ocean in Episode 8 of *Twin Peaks: The Return*, into which the nuclear bloodstream leads. The platelets dissolve, revealing this immeasurable body of liquid. This visually suggests that the basis of our bloodstream is the foundation of us all, and that foundation is the unified field of consciousness.

Lynch was a proponent of the unified field theory of consciousness and while I doubt the purple ocean in *Twin Peaks: The Return* literally meant that to Lynch, I believe that the unified field of consciousness is what Lynch perceived his version of heaven to be, and therefore, the symbolic meaning of the show's purple ocean is heaven, whether it's a place, or state, or both. For Lynch, heaven is the state of being that connects us to, and puts us in harmony with, one another.

It is our goal to achieve and experience this state, as it's a state in which bliss is the default status.

The discordant sounds of the score are eventually replaced with the calm and soothing sounds of the water and wind. The island amidst this infinite ocean is home to the black and white building in which Lynch's version of God, or gods, exist.

These godlike beings are the Fireman, aka the Giant, and Senorita Dido, and they are alerted to the detonation of the bomb through a type of cosmic alarm system. There is a decorative timelessness to the inside of this building in the same way there is a timelessness to the Red Room. There is a foreign, alien air to the space; however, like the Red Room, its 1930s Art Deco design anchors us to the world with which we are familiar. The interior design, black and white cinematography, and omission of dialogue call to mind the silent film era, an association that is reinforced when, in the next scene, the Fireman enters an old-time movie theater.

The theater's ornate interior resides somewhere between La Belle Epoque and Art Deco; however, its particulars are offset by its emptiness. There are no seats in this theater and no spectators, other than the Fireman himself. It's as though the space is his personal screening room. It is important to highlight the bygone aesthetics of the room, as these details are a manifestation of the characters that inhabit it. The aspect ratio of the theater's screen is 1.33:1, essentially a square, and it is the original aspect ratio for films in the silent era. The clever positioning of a generator with its dual pipes forms the shadow of two lines running down the left side of the screen. This is a visual reference to the optical audio track on film prints—these two lines represent what would be the left and right stereo sound channels of a projected film. However, if these lines were to represent the emission of sound, they would not be straight, but rather, they would appear as oscillating wave forms.

This is cinema in its purest form. There is no sound, simply visual language, just as filmmaking was when first invented by the Lumiere Brothers in Lyon, France in 1895. This is cinema in its infant state, before its artistry could be corrupted, before commercial interest, before studio executives and corporate boardrooms. Gods reside at the origins of their respective universes, and the gods of *Twin Peaks* reside at the beginnings of motion picture storytelling.

Yes, *Twin Peaks*, is a television show—*Fire Walk with Me* notwithstanding—but there would be no television without the invention of cinema. If cinema is Lynch's symbol for the *pure*, then television—specifically the type of television dictated by corporate interests (i.e., *Twin Peaks* Season 2)—is his symbol for the corrupt. Every idea in the universe of Lynch is buttressed by its opposite, because neither would exist without the presence of the other.

The Fireman cues up footage from earlier in the episode and projects it onto the screen. The image of the Trinity nuclear test appears and the mushroom cloud engulfs the screen. There are no new camera angles, no deviations in perspective from what we saw earlier—it's as though the Fireman is literally rewinding the episode and then fast-forwarding through its scenes. It's as though he is catching up to what the audience has been previously presented with. While doing so, Lynch provides us with another glimpse of what we witnessed a few minutes earlier. However, because the images are being played back silently, Lynch is able to alter our emotional perception of these images by omitting the discordant, and frankly terrifying, strings of "Threnody to the Victims of Hiroshima." He introduces a much more harmonious, and hopeful, piece of music into the soundtrack conducted by composer Angelo Badalamenti.

If Lynch is primarily concerned with the theme of balance, then the evil unleashed by the nuclear bomb, through which

Bob was created, must maintain equilibrium with its opposite. The Fireman and his actions represent this opposite and these actions create: Laura Palmer.

Episode 8 is not only Bob's origin story, but also Laura Palmer's. As the Experiment spews Bob from its guts, directing him, along with the other eggs, downwards, the Fireman floats upwards, above the image of Bob on the screen, and regurgitates a gold essence from his insides into the air above him. This essence is similar to the ethereal substance that rises from the little boy that Richard runs down earlier in the season. Lynch seems to equate this golden essence to something akin to the soul, or spirit, of a person. Something intangible that transcends the birth and death of an individual. In this instance, this substance is involved in the creation of a soul—not just any soul, but the soul that must counterbalance Bob—and that soul is Laura Palmer.

For Lynch, Laura Palmer is a concept, an entity that lives outside the confines of death. She is an inhabitant of the Red Room and is just as conceptual as Bob, the Fireman, the Arm, the Evolution of the Arm, and Mike. Much like the way mythical gods that visit earth are subject to mortal restraints, when Laura Palmer becomes human, she feels the pull of evil in an intrinsic, non-binary manner. She is unaware of her conceptual nature—not until she sees herself in the flickering light of the television at the end of *Fire Walk with Me*. The Fireman has created her essence and Senorita Dido takes her orb and sends it through a gold tube-like device that is able to penetrate the metafictional dimension between the reality in the scene with the non-reality of movies and television. Their joint effort leads to Laura's orb penetrating the screen and traveling toward an image of the world, presumably in the direction of the town of Twin Peaks.

This sequence fades out only to bring us back into the New Mexico desert, but this time it is eleven years later: August 5, 1956. David Lynch was fond of this year because he considered it to be the birth of rock and roll. This was the year Elvis took the world by storm; just seventeen days later, on August 22nd, Elvis began shooting his first film, *Love Me Tender*. On August 5th, The Platters' "My Prayer," which is featured prominently in this episode and later in the final episode of the series, was at the top of charts. It had even bumped Elvis.

The desert's waves of sand, which due to a high contrast of light and shadow evoke the image of a black and white zigzag floor, grow larger each time Lynch jump cuts closer to them, gradually bringing into focus a reptilian-looking egg. As the frame settles on the egg, it begins to hatch, giving birth to a creature that appears to be a cross between a frog and moth, a creature Lynch said he had come across while traveling through Yugoslavia on the Orient Express.

In what may seem like a marker of sorts, the second part of this episode begins similarly to the first: the location and time titles, an aberration of nature in a desert of white sand and a moon being eclipsed by black clouds. Lynch splits this episode intentionally, as it is his purpose to not only depict evil, but also the consequence of evil. The structure of the episode is built upon cause and effect: the evil in the first part is the cause of the violence and corruption of innocence in the second part. After the darkness descends, Lynch reestablishes the scene at a gas station, which serves as an echo of the gas station and convenience store featured in the nuclear explosion sequence. Two teenagers, a boy and girl, a young Sarah Novack [who I will refer to henceforth as Sarah Palmer for the sake of clarity], walk out from behind the building and turn into the street.

On the surface, these two kids are the archetypical young couple from the '50s, walking home from what appears to be a first date. He asks Sarah if she "liked that song," to which she replies, "I did like that song." She then spots a penny on the ground and picks it up. In an extreme close-up, Lynch shows us the penny, head's up, the year 1945 printed on it—the year of the Trinity nuclear test, the same year as the first part of this episode, the year in which modern evil was born. She rubs the imprint of President Abraham Lincoln's face and says, "It's head's up…that means it's good luck." While this moment is steeped in custom and superstition, it fits into Lynch's idea of balance, the two sides of the nickel at the heart of Bob and Mike's confrontation in the international pilot of the original show. The difference between good and bad luck is arbitrary; it's as unpredictable as a flip of the coin. The boy says, "I hope it does bring you good luck," before leaving the frame and cutting to what it does bring the viewers: a nightmare version of Abraham Lincoln.

It is at this point in the episode that the technique of intercutting becomes crucial to the metaphorical and emotional understanding of the story. Intercutting involves cutting back and forth from one continuing scene or sequence to another. Lynch employs the Kuleshov Effect, a technique that resides at the very core of film editing. The Kuleshov Effect is a cinematic theory that suggests the meaning of a shot is created when it is juxtaposed to another. With respect to scenes or sequences, the theory posits that the meaning of a scene or sequence is created when it's juxtaposed to—in this case, intercut with—another. Considering this, I argue that we can only understand the storyline of the young Sarah Palmer and the boy in light of our understanding of the nightmarish Woodsman sequence it is intercut with.

The main Woodsman, the antagonist in the sequence that is intercut with Sarah Palmer's sequence, outwardly appears to be the manifestation of Abraham Lincoln—if he were a deranged vagabond and sometimes lumberjack. The actor, Robert Broski, is a well-known Abraham Lincoln impersonator who played Lincoln exclusively on-screen in his seven productions prior to his collaboration with Lynch in *Twin Peaks: The Return*. This is no coincidence. He was sought out to play this part because of his resemblance to Lincoln. There is a connection between the "good luck" Lincoln on the penny and the "bad luck" Lincoln that Broski plays because of the Kuleshov Effect. And the connection is one of Lynchian opposites.

One storyline is the romanticized storyline, the other, the nightmare scenario—the brutal truth that bubbles beneath the surface. This Lincolnesque "Woodsman," as he is credited, floats down from the air—the opposite of the Fireman floating up earlier in the episode—lands on the ground and begins to walk through the desert. He approaches a road and accosts an older couple in a car, asking them for a light for his cigarette. The eerily modulated, and now iconic, line "Gotta light?" begins to horrifyingly reverberate in the couple's skulls, and in our skulls watching at home. The line is always pronounced the same, likely utilizing the same piece of recorded dialogue in each instance, which serves to unsettle us. It's so disturbing that we wish to not hear it again, and not only does Lynch's character say it again, he says it again the exact same way, over and over.

As the couple escapes, driving away into the dark night, Lynch cuts back to the storyline of Sarah Palmer and the boy. They are continuing their walk in the night, eventually arriving at her house. After inquiring into his relationship with another girl, Sarah is pleased to learn that he is no longer seeing her, and after feigning an objection to his request for a kiss, she allows him the pleasure. She staggers away, visibly elated, if not a little embarrassed at her elation, and walks onto the front porch of her house. The house bears an uncanny resemblance to the house that is the subject of Edward Hopper's painting *Summer Evening*. In fact, the entire final sequence of this episode references aspects of three of Hopper's paintings.

Hopper was one of Lynch's favorite painters, and it is not hard to see why: he captures the veneer of Americana, and in doing so, hints at something else, something repressed, underneath its surface. He is, in many respects, the anti-Norman Rockwell. The house and its porch are virtually identical to the house in *Summer Evening*, which features a teenage couple standing on the terrace. In the painting, the boy seems to be attempting to sweet-talk the girl, who stands with pensive eyes directed toward the ground. Perhaps it's the proposal of a kiss, like the scene in *Twin Peaks*; or perhaps it's something more.

Art historian Walter Wells writes of the painting: "Here, the adolescent yearning we see in *Second Story Sunlight*, and its hesitant assertion in *Sunlight in a Cafeteria*, have progressed to a later, tenser moment in the mating ritual—or unmating, as the case may be here—in the glare of artificial light in the night. On the porch of a wooden frame house, a young man seems to plead his case to a girl who, for the picture's everlasting instant at least, resists his entreaties."[21]

In both instances, the single source of artificial light accentuates the darkness that surrounds the house, implying that something is hidden out there: a predator, perhaps, lying in wait for an opportunity to strike. The couple in the painting, specifically the young woman, and Sarah in *Twin Peaks* appear vulnerable, if not helpless. As Sarah walks into the house, Lynch films the action over the shoulder of the boy, an intentionally voyeuristic point of view shot. It seems more appropriate for a stalker than a young lover. With the accompaniment of the eerie wind in the soundtrack, this shot conveys a feeling of impending trouble. It reverses to a medium close-up of the boy walking away, but not to where he walked from, but rather to the side toward the back of the house.

The sounds of footsteps connect the walking of the boy to the walking of the Woodsman, as Lynch intercuts to a shot of a radio station tower in the distance. The Woodsman traverses the darkness of the desert, presumably in search of his "light," and stops when he sees this rather tall tower, its height exaggerated amidst the flatness of the land in front of it. He stares at it in awe; it's as though it pulls him toward it, like it's exerting some level of control over him. Lynch frames the man's point of view of the tower in a shot that the man eventually walks into, physically connecting him with the tower itself. The shot remains static as the Woodsman walks toward the tower: the man gets smaller as the tower remains the same size; however, this produces the effect of the tower getting bigger relative to his size. The man's body stays in the center of the frame. Typically, a subject would appear to move up in the frame as they walk deeper into it; however, since he walks down a small hill, his position in frame remains the same. In essence, the slope of the hill offsets the depth cue of a rising position. It's as though he is simply shrinking and the tower is getting larger.

The juxtaposition of teenagers kissing, and assumably being aroused by the kiss, with the image of a man walking toward a growing tower appears phallic in its symbolism. Lynch is connecting the boy's desire for intimacy with Sarah to the Woodsman's lust for violence, a violence that he is about to unleash on the unsuspecting employees of the radio station.

The doo-wop tune, "My Prayer," by The Platters begins to reverberate in the soundtrack as the Woodsman approaches the station:

> *When the twilight is gone and no songbirds are singing,*
> *When the twilight is gone you come into my heart...*

As the first few lyrics of this lover's lament are sung, Lynch connects them to a montage of images: the record playing and the disc jockey playing it, a radio playing in a car mechanic's shop, a waitress cleaning the counters of a short-order diner, and finally Sarah Palmer, reclining in bed, smiling to herself, as the night breeze wafts through the open window next to her. It's as though Lynch is guiding us through living versions of Hopper paintings, particularly in the case of the diner with its resemblance to the diner of *Nighthawks*, and then inside the radio station office. As the Woodsman enters the station, the character from Hopper's *Office at Night* greets him. She is dressed in the same tight dress, her hair is fixed the same and her lips boast the

Hopper, Edward. *Office at Night*, 1940.
Walker Art Center in Minneapolis, Minnesota

Twin Peaks: The Return, Episode 8, 2017

Hopper, Edward. *Summer Evening*, 1947.
Private Collection

Twin Peaks: The Return, Episode 8, 2017

same distinct lipstick. She is positioned at the file cabinet, turned away from the man, opening a drawer, just like the woman in the painting. The majority of art critics support a sexual reading of the painting, specifically the attention the female secretary draws from the viewers. The irony is that the man in the painting, who is presumably her boss, is either unaware of the presence of his secretary or ignoring it, while the viewer usurps the attention and ogles her to him or herself. The open window plays an important role in the painting, as it not only serves as a light source, shining a rectangular spotlight on the woman and illuminating her curvy figure, but also functions as a source of mystery and tension: is there someone outside gazing at her just as we, the viewers, are gazing at her? This hint of voyeurism is brought to fruition in *Twin Peaks*, as the Woodsman passes the window and observes the secretary at the file cabinet; it is essentially the wish fulfillment of the viewer to walk inside the office, and that's what the Woodsman does.

As The Platters sing, "With the world far away and your lips close to mine," the Woodsman approaches the terrified secretary, bringing his lips closer to hers. She is helpless; they are isolated in this station, far away from town. He continues his approach and crushes the secretary's skull with his bare hands. He then turns toward the disc jockey, watching him through the glass of the studio. He approaches the man and asks for a "light" before knocking the needle off of the record, bringing "My Prayer" to a halt. The scratching of the turntable needle is broadcast over the radio, with the mechanic, the waitress and Sarah all visibly reacting. Sarah, specifically, turns her head to her left, into the direction of her open bedroom window as she looks toward the radio.

Back in the studio, the Woodsman crushes the disc jockey's head, digging the tips of his fingers into his skull, as he grabs the microphone with his other hand. While holding onto the man, he begins to recite his poem on the air:

This is the water
And this is the well.
Drink full and descend.

The horse is the white of the eyes and dark within.

Much like his repetition of "Gotta light," he recites these lines over and over, triggering those listening to the broadcast to fall asleep, including Sarah. As Sarah lies down and closes her eyes, the frog-moth is seen crawling toward, and eventually through, her open window. Lynch frames Sarah from the waist up, much like Elvis was filmed on Ed Sullivan, omitting what's below. The shadow of her curtain dances in the background as the ominous wind blows in and the frog-moth enters the frame. The creature meticulously opens her mouth and crawls inside. She swallows as the Woodsman recites, "Drink full and descend..."

As the frog-moth makes its way through Sarah's insides, Lynch cuts back to the studio where the Woodsman continues his mantra into the microphone. His recitation becomes more forceful as he increases his viselike grip on the top of the disc jockey's head, and his eyes roll back in orgasmic fashion as he cracks the back of the man's cranium. Blood begins to pour out from his victim's skull and we see this through the opening in the man's headphone band, the form of which appears symbolically vaginal. As the blood splashes to the floor, the Woodsman removes his fingers from the man and leaves, accomplishing what he set out to do, stealing the light away from these innocent people. The Woodsman leaves the frame in total darkness as he walks into the night toward the neighing of a distant, unseen horse.

If we are to view the moments after Sarah Palmer returns home in relation to the metaphors of the frog-moth and the Woodsman's carnage at the radio station, we could decipher the events as the symbolic, perhaps even literal, rape of Sarah. We may interpret the sequence as the following: the boy is attracted to Sarah, asks for a kiss, wants more, she leaves, entering her house; he walks around the house, finds an open window, crawls inside, and has sexual intercourse with her. The frog-moth is the manifestation of his desire, the evil that hatched in the desert, and if it remains unchecked, it can take control of him, or us. Instead of watching the boy's assault on Sarah Palmer, we witness the brutality the Woodsman perpetrates on his victims.

Through these grisly images, Lynch conveys the feeling of Sarah's trauma expressionistically, rather than depicting the realism of the assault. David Lynch was not a realist; he was a surrealist with expressionistic tendencies. The frog-moth, this aberration of nature—which calls to mind the biological mutations that can result from nuclear contamination—enters her, but in reality, it is the boy's penis, foreign and alien, that enters her. As the Woodsman's eyes go white, rolling back into his brow, the boy orgasms, the blood released from the DJ's cracked head representing the blood released from Sarah's broken hymen.

While this interpretation may, at first glance, seem provocative, it aligns with the subject matter and subtext Lynch navigates in *Twin Peaks*. Rape and childhood trauma are at the heart of *Twin Peaks*; they are the very reason *Twin Peaks* exists as a show. Laura Palmer was raped, abused, and ultimately murdered by her father. This is a show about rape and abuse and Episode 8 is its origin story. If the first half of the episode depicts the origin of good and evil in the show, the second half of the show depicts the modus operandi of good and evil. In other words, how do these forces function and what are their intents?

Their target is Sarah Palmer, which makes sense because she is the origin of the corporeal Laura Palmer. One of the main subjects *Twin Peaks* explores is the intergenerational aspect of abuse, specifically child abuse. In most cases, child abusers were abused as children themselves. The abuse is self-perpetuating. In Episode 3 of Season 2, Leland Palmer tells Agent Cooper and Sheriff Truman that he knows the man in the wanted sketch for Laura's murder. He says, "When I was a little boy, my grandfather had a summer home up on Pearl Lakes. We used to go there every year." He explains to Cooper that there was a white house next to them and that's where "he" lived. The name was Robertson (son of Robert). "He used to flick matches at me," Leland recalled. "He'd say, 'You want to play with fire little boy?'" Leland then takes out a match, lights it and flicks it exactly the way he described; he did it just like it was done to him, which speaks directly to the idea of generational abuse. The flicking of this match is learned behavior, just like the abuse he perpetrates against his daughter.

Violence begets violence is a notion that Lynch's filmmaking explores, and through exploring, rails against. This is at the heart of the scene in *Fire Walk with Me* when Laura Palmer takes the owl ring, compelling her father/Bob to kill her. This is a moment of empowerment, rather than surrender. Laura takes the ring in an effort to prevent Bob from inhabiting her and therefore continuing the cycle of abuse—if Laura were to survive, she would likely exhibit abusive, violent, and criminal behavior toward others. The cycle is corrosive, and while Laura's death is tragic, it would also be tragic if she were to have survived and continued to infect those around her with this generational, and very much contagious, disease.

Leland Palmer, while dying in Episode 9 of Season 2, explicitly reveals how he was abused as a child: "I was just a boy. I saw him in my dreams. He asked if I wanted to play. He opened me. And I invited him and he came inside me. When he was inside, I didn't know. And when he was gone, I couldn't remember. He made me do things. Terrible things. He said he wanted lives. He wanted others, others that they could use, like they used me. They wanted Laura. But she was strong; she fought him. She wouldn't let him in. She said she'd die before she'd let him. Then they made me kill her." Laura breaks the cycle of abuse and the way she does it is through Christlike self-sacrifice.

This is the very reason Lynch chooses to portray Laura as much more than a flesh and blood human being. He has brought this character to life through her death. She transcends the trappings of commonplace cause and effect—because her actions result in her death. For these actions to be thought of as heroic, they must have consequences that extend beyond everyday mortal boundaries. They must extend toward the angelic, toward the supernatural, toward the godhead. Laura Palmer is not just a prom queen to Lynch; she is an angel, quite literally. She is one of the building blocks of good in Lynch's universe, just as Bob is a building block of evil.

In Episode 8 of Season 3, Lynch implicitly depicts Sarah Palmer as being infected by the same evil that has infected Leland. Leland's dying words can almost be used verbatim to describe Sarah's encounter with the frog-moth, "He opened me. And I invited him and he came inside me." If we are to use Lynch's metaphor of Bob to describe Leland's abuse, and his subsequent abuse of others, it is not a far leap to propose that the frog-moth is the metaphor he uses to depict Sarah's abuse, and subsequent abuse—or the willful denial of abuse—of others. If Sarah was abused and raped herself, it is much more likely that she would fall victim to, and find herself complicit in, future instances of abuse. Such a circumstance would also serve as common ground for Sarah and Leland, as they are cut from the same cloth, per se. The evil that was unleashed through the Trinity nuclear test thrives within the unholy trinity of the one who kills, the one who dies, and the one who watches. This unholy trinity, as I mentioned earlier, manifests itself within the triangular relationship of Leland, Laura, and Sarah.

Lynch symbolically links both Leland's and Sarah's crimes against Laura through the framed photograph of her homecoming queen portrait, an image that ends virtually every episode of the original series. It is the glue that connects each episode together. In Season 3, this is the image that opens each episode. In Season 1, Leland dances with this framed photograph. Sarah tries to wrestle it away only to break it, causing Leland to cut his hand and bleed all over it. This connects to the scene in Season 3 after Cooper saves Laura. In response to this changing of preordained history, Sarah Palmer, as the manifestation of Judy, breaks the frame of the same photo of Laura in anger; she abuses it, perpetrating violence against it.

This photograph serves as the memory of Laura's idealization; it is Laura as earthly angel, the perfect prom queen and exemplar of the community. Just like the owls, this photograph

is not what it seems, just as Cooper discovers when he "saves" Laura from the timeline of her death. The pursuit of perfection on earth, a perfection that is depicted in this photograph, is unattainable, not only for Laura, but also for us. There are forces beyond the perfection of this photograph that will continue to influence Laura and steer her down the path of abuse, and—in the case of her reincarnation as Carrie Page—of violence and murder.

The cycle of abuse is simple: Leland learns to rape by being raped and Sarah learns to ignore rape by being raped. Laura was born into a loop of abuse, rape and violence, a loop that is represented by the brutal images of boxing matches and animals slaughtering one another that Sarah watches over and over again on her television at home, the home in which Laura was raised.

Cooper, and by extension the audience, must "kill two birds with one stone," as the Fireman reiterates in Episode 1 of Season 3. The two birds are Laura's parents, Leland (Bob) and Sarah (Judy), as their conjoined active and passive evil must be roundly condemned. Seasons 1 and 2 brought Leland to justice and Season 3 holds Sarah to account. The stone is the death of Laura Palmer, because through her death, this television show was born, and it is this show that brings to light the reprehensible behavior of her parents.

Laura Palmer never had a chance, but Lynch believed that we can help give others one.

WILLIAM DICKERSON

EPISODES 15-17: THE ERSATZ SHOW

Season 3's qualifier in its title, *The Return,* alludes to more than just one thing. Of course, it is a reference to *Twin Peaks* returning to television. The plot involves Cooper returning to Twin Peaks, both the town and the show, and the fictional reality of Lynch's world, after being trapped for 25 years inside the Red Room. Mark Frost has said that *Twin Peaks: The Return* is also modeled after Homer's *Odyssey,* in which the presumed dead Greek hero Odysseus returns home after fighting in the Trojan War, a journey that lasts ten years. If Lynch is primarily concerned with the theme, namely achieving balance between the forces of good and evil, Frost is primarily concerned with the plot. The plot of the third season hinges around the idea of *returning,* specifically, the notion of returning to reality.

In Episode 2 of Season 3, the good Dale Cooper leaves the Red Room, but not in the manner he is supposed to, due to the sabotage of the evil Mr. C. As the good Cooper roams the curtained hallways of the lodge, the zigzag floor begins to shift under his feet, its white and black lines rising up and down, throwing Cooper physically off balance. The floor splits, revealing a pool of choppy liquid, and the electrified tree-like doppelganger of the Evolution of the Arm screams, "non-exist-ent!" Cooper falls into the liquid, which then seems to transform into the night sky and his body skydives through it amidst the stars. He eventually ends up in the glass box we saw at the beginning of the season's first episode. It's quite possible that Mr. C, the proprietor of this box, built this device as a mechanism to catch his doppelganger the moment he left the Red Room. Ironically, however, the young man hired to monitor the box is not there to witness this moment. He is not there to witness Cooper float into it and make his presence known behind the glass. Rather, the young man is outside the room, tending to a young woman in whom he has a romantic interest; Cooper is left staring at the empty couch where his spectator should be sitting and paying attention.

Back in the first episode, we are introduced to the young man sitting in front of this box, an enormous glass enclosure that features a tube in the back of it that leads to an opening to the outside. This box, and the spectatorship of it, is a clear metaphor for television, which is also known as "the tube," a name derived from the cathode-ray tube inside of the appliance that shoots electrons toward a phosphor-coated glass screen. This young man is sitting and waiting for something to happen through the glass, which is reminiscent of *Twin Peaks* fans sitting and waiting for the return of the show on their television sets. We are all waiting for the same thing to appear through the glass: Special Agent Dale Cooper. However, we missed him; more specifically, the new generation of television watchers—those less interested in Netflix, and more interested in chilling—missed him. The notion of a television character not being seen on television is perfectly in line with the sentiment of the Evolution of the Arm's doppelganger: the character is "non-exist-ent!" A television character only exists when someone watches that character on the screen. Otherwise, the character ceases to exist.

It is interesting, but also not surprising, to note that the last time prior to *The Return* that Lynch worked within the world of *Twin Peaks* was when he made *Fire Walk with Me*, a movie that begins and ends with the motif of the television. Therefore, beginning the third season with a visual metaphor of watching television makes perfect sense. Lynch wants to remind us that *Twin Peaks* is, and always was, a work of metafiction, and the simple fact that we've been sitting on our couches waiting for it to come back to the air has been incorporated into the show itself.

In Episode 3, Cooper completes his freefall and finds himself in a room on the edge of the purple ocean. As I suggested previously, this purple ocean is representative of the unified field of consciousness, the closest thing to heaven that Lynch could depict in the show. For Lynch, this field is the foundation of all human beings, and in regard to the world of the show, it is the foundation of all its characters and the origin of its storylines. It is the source of interconnectedness between people, places and circumstances, and this is where the character of Naido, played by Nae Yuuki, resides. Cooper asks Naido, "Where is this?" She cannot speak and is unable to answer him. If the purple ocean is representative of the consciousness of the show, one might think of her residence, a cavernous stone room with a circular couch and fireplace, as a metaphor for a television show's writers' room, or in this instance, the creative minds of David Lynch and Mark Frost. This purple-lit place is the engine of the show; it's what generates and organizes its ideas. We know this because it features electrical sockets in the walls that serve as literal pathways to specific episodes.

The sockets I am referring to display the numbers 3 and 15. Cooper is drawn to socket number 15; however, Naido jumps between him and the socket, vehemently warning him not to approach it. She gestures a cutting motion across her neck to, presumably, indicate the result could be death or a fate just as grave. Simultaneously, a malevolent entity from outside the room begins to bang on a steel door, denting it with its force. The entire room sounds as though it will collapse upon itself if Cooper were to use this socket. Naido stops him, leading him up a ladder to the roof, which reveals that they are no longer surrounded by purple water, but rather the darkness of outer space. She then pulls a lever to a generator—similar to the Man in the Planet in *Eraserhead* pulling his lever—that engages a strong electrical current, propelling her off the top and into the abyss below.

When Cooper climbs back down inside of the stone room, the purple hue that saturated the image before has lifted, skin tones have returned to normal and the actress who played Ronette Pulaski, Phoebe Augustine, sits in front of the fireplace. Cooper sees a socket numbered 3, which he begins to approach, and is encouraged to do so by Augustine's character, who is credited as American Girl. As he feels the socket's electric charge, the American Girl says to him, "When you get there…you will already be there." Cooper moves closer to the socket and it begins to pull him into it head first.

These sockets serve as portals to specific episodes, in this case, Episodes 15 and 3. Initially, Cooper is drawn to Episode 15, as that is the episode in which he inserts a metal fork into an electrical socket and begins his transformation from the debilitated Dougie Jones back to his old self. In essence, by skipping ahead to Episode 15, Cooper bypasses the entire Dougie Jones storyline, which he, and arguably some members of the audience, would wish to do. If this location that sits atop the purple sea of consciousness is a place in which all knowledge is known, then the Cooper inside this place must be aware of the show and what happens in each episode. He is in the metafictional writers' room, after all. Equipped with this knowledge, he must realize that he cannot skip right to Episode 15 because Episodes 3 to 14 already exist, which echo the American Girl's words, "When you get there...you will already be there." The season has already been shot and his character, in one form or another, is present in all of the episodes. Her words also, more literally, refer to the fact that his *tulpa* (or copy), Dougie Jones, "is already there," and that, essentially, he will be replacing him. From a metafictional standpoint, if Cooper were to skip ahead to Episode 15, he would be cutting out Episodes 3 to 14, leaving an editorial void in the series. This is a result that may very well be indicated by Naido when she mimes the gesture of cutting her own throat.

Lynch was meticulous when it came to symbolism and numbers were a part of his meticulousness. He was acutely aware of the audience's desire to revisit the old show, namely, to see Cooper escape the Red Room and right all the wrongs he can in the "real" world of *Twin Peaks*. Lynch knew much of the audience was tuning in to see Agent Cooper awaken and proclaim, as he does in Episode 16, "I am the FBI," and part of the reason Dougie Jones exists as a character is to subvert this desire and the expectation that results from such a longing.

This is the same desire that resulted in the premature revealing of Laura Palmer's killer in Season 2. It is the desire that killed Lynch's proverbial "golden goose." I don't think it is coincidence that it was the 15th episode of the original run of *Twin Peaks* in which the killer, Leland Palmer, was revealed. The desire of the network, and much of the audience at the time, was to skip ahead and reveal the killer sooner in the series. Episode 3 of *Twin Peaks: The Return* is colored by this previous experience, and since Lynch is in control of this writers' room, he refuses to let Cooper, and by extension, the audience, bypass most of the series to get to the point where their impatience wants them to get. There is an aspect to Dougie Jones in which Lynch is poking a little bit of fun at his viewers, playing with their longing and testing their patience; however, Lynch's love for this character, as is the case with most of his characters, is sincere. In fact, it seems clear that the show that is *Twin Peaks: The Return* is encapsulated between Episodes 1 through 15, and the remaining episodes are something different altogether.

Balance was critical to David Lynch and Episodes 1 through 15 exhibit a balance between the unabashed evil of Mr. C. and the inherent innocence of Dougie Jones. Once the good Cooper is restored, the show resolves itself in just about an episode, which is wholly unrealistic, yet perfectly reasonable in the world of network television. For Lynch, Episode 3 is representative of the real show, a show of balanced opposites: as dark as the darkest parts of the show are, Lynch seeks to genuinely convey a sense of happiness and humor through Dougie's storyline. For those who grow impatient with the storyline, it is their baser instincts that pull them away from it and into the direction of Mr. C's story. The viewer's experience of Dougie's storyline should be the diametric opposite of their experience of Mr. C's. Both experiences are equally valuable, as they can only exist in parallel to the other, and those who discount Dougie's storyline as insignificant to the show miss the point entirely. The end of Episode 15, and the following Episodes 16 and 17, are representative of the *ersatz* show—the show in which good unequivocally wins, Bob and the evil he represents are defeated, and everything is tied up into a neat bow, just the kind of bow network executives love to tie on television.

The moment Dougie sticks the backend of his fork into an

electrical socket in Episode 15, and the power goes out, the lights go out on the entire season up until that moment. This is emphasized in the following scene when Margaret Lanterman, the Log Lady, calls Deputy Hawk and tells him that she is dying. This moment carries particular resonance since Catherine Coulson, who plays the Log Lady, died from terminal cancer two days after shooting this scene. Catherine was one of Lynch's longest collaborators and oldest friends, having been one of the few at his side during the production of *Eraserhead*. Lynch was aware Catherine did not have much longer to live and directed her in these scenes over Skype inside her home. When she states, "I'm dying," this rings true in myriad ways. Both Catherine and her character are dying in this scene, a scene that follows the death of Dougie Jones, a scene that follows the end of balanced opposites and ushers forth the quick, and seemingly happy, resolution to the series. When Hawk gathers everyone in the sheriff's station together to share the news of Margaret's passing, it's as though he shares the news of the show's demise, which translates to their demise as characters. How can there be a *Twin Peaks* without the Log Lady?

The end of Episode 15 is fashioned as a non sequitur. Non sequiturs were Lynch's signature flourish and a staple of surrealist art, but while this scene seemingly does not relate to what comes before, or after, in the plot, dream logic still governs it and a concrete subtextual connection to the material surrounding this moment exists. We find ourselves back in the Roadhouse's *Bang Bang Bar* watching and listening to the evening's performance, in this case, "Axolotl" by The Veils, and do so through the point of view of a female character we have not met before and will not meet again. This woman is the very personification of a non sequitur. She sits alone in a booth, meek with large-lens glasses—glasses similar to the Log Lady's glasses—when two bikers in leather jackets descend upon her. Addressing their stares of non-verbal intimidation, she states, "I'm waiting for someone." The bikers have no desire to let her wait and proceed to pull her up by her arms and place her on the ground next to the booth. The camera remains at her eye level, close to the ground, solidifying her point of view, as she crawls between the legs of dancing spectators. Lynch begins to rapidly intercut between the band on stage and this woman. As the singer shouts, "Oh my soul… losing control," the character begins to yell uncontrollably—it is a primal scream that goes completely unnoticed by those around her, a scream that segues into the darkness of the end credits.

Lynch harnesses the frustration that the audience has been experiencing waiting for the real Cooper to show up in this scene. It is a reflection of our own expectations and the subversion of those expectations. Dougie has just attempted to escape himself through the electrical socket, but instead of magically transforming into the Cooper we have all been waiting for him to morph into, we are presented with the possibility that he may have irreparably harmed, or perhaps even killed, himself. This line of thought is congruous with the collective nightmare of waiting for someone that ultimately doesn't show up, the nightmare this woman in the Bang Bang Bar is experiencing. The subtextual significance of this scene is grounded in the idea that what we expect to show up is not what actually shows up. Like the audience's collective desire for Laura Palmer's killer to be revealed in the original series, our desire to dispense with Dougie Jones and replace him with the Cooper we're familiar with—the perfect, irreproachable, metaphysical crime fighter we know and love—destroys the show itself, a terrifying realization that this woman's scream is a symbolic reaction to.

After this scream, and following the end credits, the show transitions into a program that is seemingly designed by metafictional network executives. In Episode 16, a series of resolutions—the types of resolutions that are historically verboten in Lynch's work—avalanche toward us: Richard, perhaps the most detestable character in the show, is brutally murdered by his father, Mr. C; Hutch and Chantal, the show's resident hitman and hitwoman, are randomly killed via *deus ex machina* in a firefight with a heavily armed accountant; Diane reveals herself as a tulpa working in concert with Mr. C, who is consequently killed by the FBI; and following a performance by Eddie Vedder, arguably the most famous musician featured in the show's musical sequences, Audrey Horne finally leaves the purgatory of her home to visit the Bang Bang Bar and perform her signature *Twin Peaks* dance as her pièce de résistance. All of these moments are simply sprinkles on top of the donut that is the most seemingly significant event of the series: Cooper awakens from his coma and is, finally, back to his old, iconic self. Vedder's lyrics mirror Cooper's awakening:

> *Now it's gone, gone*
> *And I am who I am.*
> *Who I was I will never be again.*

These lyrics contain a dual meaning, as many of the song lyrics Lynch employed in his work do. Cooper is no longer Dougie Jones; he has been freed from the shackles of this character. It also means that the Cooper we are being presented with post-Dougie, the Cooper we think we know and recognize, is not the same Cooper we knew from the original series. That Cooper is impossible to recapture. Kyle MacLachlan is also significantly older than when he first played the role, so Cooper can't be the same—nor can any of the other characters. It's not just the plot that's changed them; it's the wrinkles too. This Cooper is an idealized version of what we, as an audience, want Cooper to be, and as we'll see later, in reality, this version of Cooper may not even exist at all.

An entire series worth of storylines are brought to a close in this episode and wrapped up nice and neat. They are the types of tidy resolutions that are antithetical to Lynch's artistic sensibility and his affinity for open endings. In fact, this episode is so non-Lynchian that it seems to be a comment on Lynch himself. Lynch appears to be superficially copying, and paying homage to, the old show in this episode and the following episode, which perhaps reflects the wish fulfillment of the audience. Is Lynch simply giving his audience what they want? Or, more likely, Lynch wants the audience to believe they're getting what they want, only to make it clear in the final two episodes that what they think they want is not what they want, or even should want. There is an aspect of this part of the season in which Lynch is, without question, commenting on "fan favoritism" and how such an endeavor leads to emptiness. This is not the real show, as much as the audience wants it to be; it is simply an echo of its former self.

Perhaps when Audrey's moment of reverie in The Roadhouse is interrupted and she finds herself trapped inside a white room looking in horror at herself in a mirror, this is a hint that everything we've just witnessed is not real. It is what it is: reverie. Audrey's dance scene is about as made-for-fans as *Twin*

Peaks gets and Lynch exploits our enjoyment of it when he unceremoniously pulls us out of it. Dreams, like nightmares, do not last; we eventually must wake up to reality. The white void that she finds herself in is the emptiness the audience is left with after watching Episode 16.

In Episode 17, the tone and convenient plot mechanics of the previous episode continue in the same manner. When Mr. C is captured by the Fireman and transported to the sheriff station's parking lot, he turns and looks at the station, muttering under his breath, "What is this?" His words are filled with trepidation and building anger, as he begins to realize he has been set up. Lynch is hitting the conventions of the crime show hard on the nose here. This is the criminal's showdown with the law, and of course, the law will prevail. In this case, Lynch invokes the television trope of the off-screen greenhorn, Lucy, who shoots the bad guy, Mr. C, in the nick of time to save the good guy, Sheriff Truman. What unfolds in this scene is the kind of soap opera contrivance that's more suitable for an episode of *Twin Peaks'* show-within-a-show, *Invitation to Love*, than *Twin Peaks* itself. Andy gathers everyone in the station into the Sheriff's office as Bob materializes from Mr. C's torso and Cooper gets there at just the right moment for the final confrontation. We know what happens after that. Freddy Sykes fulfills the destiny connected to his green-gloved hand and destroys Bob, sending the shards of his orb into the ether. Everyone—cops, FBI, gangsters—gathers around Agent Cooper as he explains what's actually going on. While Cooper addresses everyone around him, a large close-up of Cooper's face is superimposed onto the screen. We are presented with a double image of Cooper: 1) The Cooper walking and talking in the scene; and 2) The Cooper we saw at the very beginning of the series sitting and speaking with the Fireman.

What we're watching on TV has become what Cooper himself is watching on TV; Lynch has just made his main character, and the audience's faithful proxy, self-aware of the television show he, himself, stars in. The show that he's watching could not feel any more like a television show, and Lynch designed it this way, embracing the tropes of neat plot resolution and fulfillment of the love story, specifically Naido's transforming into Diane and Cooper reuniting with her through a kiss. The goings-on encompass the air of the ridiculous.

After peering at the clock on the wall, which remains stuck at 2:53, the superimposed version of Cooper states in slow motion, "We live inside a dream," acknowledging that they are characters inside of a television show. In fact, shortly after Cooper says this, the editor cuts to David Lynch as Gordon Cole surrounded by his characters; this television show is, in a sense, David Lynch's dream and they're starring in it. The superimposition of Cooper is the reflection of him realizing the unreality of the story in which he plays a major role.

At the start of Episode 1, we see the Fireman sitting across from Cooper, and it is filmed in black and white. The superimposition of Cooper's face in Episode 17 is also in black and white. There is a knowingness that exudes from this superimposition; it's as though he has already watched these proceedings in Sheriff Truman's office, which makes sense, as the scene in the beginning of Episode 1 presents us with a Cooper who is aware of details that arise later in the series. In this initial scene, the Fireman asks Cooper to remember the following: 1) 430; 2) Richard and Linda; and 3) Two birds with one stone. To which Cooper responds: "I understand."

The only conceivable way that Cooper could understand these statements is if he had lived, or watched, the events of the series all the way up until the final episode. Cooper is, assumably, sitting with the Fireman in his castle on the purple sea. We later discover that at the heart of this castle is a movie theater that can project parts of the series—the series this scene itself is a part of—in a non-linear fashion. Just like the minute hand of the clock at 2:53, the show can move forwards and backwards in time on this movie screen, enlightening those who view it. In essence, Lynch begins the series with the very end of the series; he starts it with a Cooper who has just finished watching the series, perhaps in the Fireman's theater, and has thusly accumulated the requisite knowledge to state, "I understand," in response to the Fireman's advice.

The beginning and end of the show are structured similarly to the infinity symbol that appears next to the teakettle-esque generator that has become Phillip Jeffries, the elusive FBI agent played by David Bowie in *Fire Walk with Me*, at The Dutchman's Lodge. Watching *Twin Peaks: The Return* is not a linear experience; in fact, it may be appropriate to say that one must return to watch it again in order to truly understand it as Agent Cooper understands it. This is also not a surprise, as most, if not all, of David Lynch's work requires multiple viewings to fully absorb and understand the nuances of his underlying themes.

After the television reunion and climactic defeat of evil that takes place in Sheriff Truman's office conclude, Cooper walks into a dark basement boiler room not dissimilar to the basement of the hospital where Mike and Bob confront each other at the end of the international pilot of the original series. He is accompanied by Diane and Gordon; however, he cautions that he must walk alone through the door at the back of the room, a door that he opens with the key belonging to his old room at the Great Northern Hotel, room number 315. As he walks through the threshold, he stops and turns to Diane and Gordon and says, "I'll see you at the curtain call," making another reference to the unreality that is the show in which they're starring.

It is quite possible that part of Cooper's awakening is also an awakening of self-awareness. Self-awareness of being a character on a show and fulfilling that character's duty on the show.

As Cooper traverses the darkness that lies on the other side of the door, Mike approaches him, further connecting this scene to the final scene in the international pilot. Mike recites the same poem that Bob recited in this similar situation, underscoring the fact that Bob is no longer there. *Twin Peaks* has looped back to the beginning and erased Bob, which may have planted the seed in Cooper's head to return just prior to Laura's murder and erase that cataclysmic event from the show's history. Cooper's job as an FBI agent is not only to solve crimes, but also to prevent them, and if he's discovered a new technique to accomplish the latter, he will surely utilize it.

Mike leads him through the ethereal pathways of the convenience store stairs and The Dutchman's Lodge to the generator that embodies Phillip Jeffries. The Dutchman's Lodge is the roadside motel where Teresa Banks, Ronette Pulaski, and Laura Palmer worked as prostitutes. Cooper provides Jeffries with a date, February 23rd, 1989, the night Laura was killed. Jeffries asks Cooper to say hello to Gordon and that "he will remember the unofficial version," alluding to the soon-to-be-changed history of the show sans the death of Laura. Jeffries conjures an image of the symbol from the owl ring, a design that morphs into an infinity loop, inside of which Jeffries locates the date that Cooper is looking for.

Cooper and the audience are then transported via "electricity," as Mike puts it, to the scene in *Fire Walk with Me* when Laura sneaks out of her house. Her father is watching from a window as she hops on James' bike and rides to the intersection of Sparkwood and 21. Lynch specifically uses the film itself as the world that Cooper is transported into. He does not reshoot these scenes and create an entirely new perspective through which to view Laura and James in these moments;

he only supplements the film's preexisting footage with new shots of Cooper watching in the woods from behind a tree. He adds this point of view of Cooper to the scene in a manner that makes us rethink the scene we thought we knew from the movie. The meticulous preservation of *Fire Walk with Me's* shots, only augmenting what is absolutely necessary to the story, seems to imply that while Cooper's actions are changing the film and, subsequently, the universe of the show, he is not changing anything in the reality outside of this story.

In reality, there is no Laura Palmer, of course; she is a character played by the actress Sheryl Lee. Furthermore, if the show were to change, and essentially, erase her death from its existence, the "unofficial version" still remains. The original *Twin Peaks* continues to exist in the world, which includes Laura's death—the new show will forever be a palimpsest under which traces of the old show are destined to seep through.

Laura's death generated echoes within the *Twin Peaks* universe, echoes that cross between worlds, parallel or otherwise. These echoes cannot be erased entirely. Whether we refer to them as parallel timelines or alternative universes, *Twin Peaks*—particularly the third season—introduced these possibilities in its narrative. For example, "The Zone" that the character Bill Hastings, played by Matthew Lillard, subscribes to and that Gordon Cole saw through to moments before Bill's head explodes is presented as real in the story. Therefore, if a character were to change the events in one timeline, it begs the question: how does that change affect the other timelines, if at all?

When Agent Cooper intercepts Laura in the woods, preventing her from meeting Jacques, Leo, and Ronette, and subsequently saving her from her death, he is actively rewriting the course trajectory of the show. The inclination within Cooper that he can save Laura from her fate is simultaneously an act of hubris and a natural, and indispensable, part of his character. The good Cooper, that is to say the Cooper who is not Mr. C. or Dougie Jones, is emblematic of the yang, the white side of the yin and yang symbol. He is without black, whereas Mr. C is emblematic of the yin, the black side of the symbol. Mr. C is without white.

It is impossible for the good Cooper to recognize this as an act of hubris, because this version of Cooper is the epitome of idealism. His idealism, and his training as an officer of the law, do not permit him to question the ramifications of saving someone's life. Saving someone's life is the goal in and of itself. The notion that Laura's death, specifically her willingness to die, may have contributed to the greater good is a concept that Agent Cooper cannot accept. His character was not written to accept such a thing and is consequently handicapped by the writers' intentions—intentions that underscore the idea that it's more important to focus on the balance between good and evil rather than on one side or the other. The achievement of one hundred percent good is an impossibility; however, for the good Cooper, it is not, and therein lies his fatal flaw.

Even someone as inherently virtuous as Cooper is disadvantaged if he is blind to the malevolence that he, and other people as seemingly good as him, are capable of. Even if what they are capable of is a mere fraction of the bad, it is still a fraction that exists and must be recognized in order to achieve balance.

When Cooper reaches out to Laura in the woods and she takes his hand, Lynch uses shots from the pilot episode to cut to Laura's dead body, wrapped in plastic, lying on the shore adjacent to the giant log. The image of her body next to the log dematerializes along with the sound of electrical arcing. When Lynch cuts back to Cooper and Laura in the woods, the black and white cinematography begins to transform into color, literally bringing the life back into Laura's crimson cheeks. After Cooper tells her they're going "home," leading her deeper into the woods, the audience is guided through the opening images of the pilot without Laura Palmer's dead body—officially rewriting the series *Twin Peaks*, as we knew it. However, as I mentioned, what is being rewritten is a story under which the traces of what came before remain, and one of these traces refuses to be rewritten—and that trace is Judy.

As Lynch cuts away from his re-imagined pilot episode, from a shot in which Pete Martell is serenely fishing, having never encountered Laura's dead body, he introduces us to a shot inside Sarah Palmer's living room. It's a location that now exists in a purgatory of sorts between two worlds: the world in which Laura Palmer was killed and the world in which Cooper saved her. Sarah Palmer groans off-screen; she sounds like a wounded animal, like one of the animals she regularly watches being slain on her television. The iconic prop photograph of Laura as homecoming queen is present in the shot, standing beside an overflowing ashtray of cigarette butts and a bottle of prescription pills.

Just as our eyes are drawn to the photo of Laura, so are Sarah's as she enters the scene from behind the camera. She heads straight toward the photo, picks it up and walks it to the other side of the room. It's as though she wants us to stop looking at it, that she knows it is the object of our attention and she wants to destroy our connection to it. It is, in fact, our connection to the photo—an image that represents the series that *Twin Peaks* was before Cooper rewrote it—that keeps Laura's story alive. Sarah begins to stab at the photo with an empty liquor bottle, shattering the glass in the frame. In effect, Sarah's destruction of the picture frame can be read as Judy's desire to kill Laura all over again. In the previous story, Bob, using Leland Palmer as a host, killed Laura. However, understanding that Laura has been saved and Bob has been extinguished from this reality, Judy, using Sarah Palmer as a host, is compelled to finish the job.

Sarah is not literally killing Laura again by repeatedly stabbing her photograph, but symbolically, it is clear that evil still has Laura in its sights. It doesn't matter that Agent Cooper saved her from her famous death because, for there to be a show in the first place, Laura has to die. David Lynch, as the ostensible god of *Twin Peaks*, had already written, filmed, and broadcast her death, and while he rewrites the event in Episode 17, her troubled life is just too powerful to erase from whatever timeline she ends up in. From the moment her character was conceived and Laura Palmer, the idea, was born, her path ended in death. As we witness at the end of *Fire Walk with Me*, this is because she can only be redeemed through death. If Laura were a living, breathing human being there might be other paths toward redemption, as death shouldn't be the goal in and of itself in anyone's life. However, Laura is not a living, breathing human being. She's an ideal; she is David Lynch's angel, his "golden goose," in his words—she is a figurative specter whose presence hangs over the entire series like an awning succumbing to the weight of the snow that has accumulated on top of it. The snow will eventually either fall or melt over the side, or tear through the canvas itself and plummet to the ground below.

David Lynch's creation, Laura Palmer, as we've previously established, is no mere mortal. By way of bloodline, we can stipulate that her parents operate on a similar figurative level, a distinction made clear by their respective manifestations of evil: Bob and Judy. This idea is further emphasized by the fact that Sarah Palmer is immune to the change in history that Agent Cooper has seemingly caused. She remembers the original storyline; she remembers her daughter's part in that storyline, her husband's part in that storyline, and most significantly, her own part in that storyline. Lynch makes some bold editorial choices to highlight Sarah's character having one foot in one storyline and one foot in another. He manipulates the temporal nature of the scene, in rather schizophrenic fashion, moving Sarah forwards and backwards in time as she attacks the photo, dropping and adding film frames, underscoring the notion that she, as Judy, exists beyond the boundaries of corporeal existence—corporeal existence as it is presented in the show.

Lynch shows the glass in the frame breaking and then merging back together as though unbreaking. While the notion that Judy remains even though Laura has been saved is disconcerting, the fact that this action pushes back against Judy, battling her intentions and putting that broken frame back together after she's broken it, gives us hope. Perhaps Agent Cooper has solved the problem after all.

As Cooper continues to guide Laura through the woods, diverting her away from her impending death, he turns back when he hears the sound that the Fireman told him to listen to in the first episode of Season 3: the sound of a needle coming to the end of a spinning vinyl record. This sound is an important marker. It is the noise associated with Maddy being murdered

by Leland in the original series, as he played a record for Sarah after he drugged her. Therefore, when the sound emerges in Season 3, it carries with it an overtly negative connotation. It is also, generally speaking, the sound of a type of sonic purgatory. When a vinyl record comes to its end on a turntable, the record itself keeps spinning and the needle locks into a looped groove. This looped groove is most often empty, its purpose to keep the stylus from drifting onto the label and damaging its tip. However, a needle traveling through an empty groove still emits sound, usually crackling and scratching, the noise it picks up when bouncing from one side of the groove and back to the other. In an effort to make this mechanism more musical and idiosyncratic, bands in the past have incorporated sound into this empty space, most notably The Beatles on their record, *Sgt. Pepper's Lonely Hearts Club Band*. They used it as a means of creating an infinite loop of sound in the dead wax of their record, either as a way to continue to entertain their listeners or to alert them that it's time to turn the record over. In either instance, as the stylus runs through this groove, the sound is never-ending.

The idea of a locked "looped" groove is essential to the meaning of this scene in the woods. The form and function of this mechanism is closely connected to the meaning behind an infinity symbol. The infinity symbol that Phillip Jeffries displays to Cooper may have been a warning to him. Cooper may believe he can change history by saving Laura Palmer, but history is always destined to repeat itself—if not in the primary storyline then, as we'll see later, in a storyline that's parallel to it. This further reinforces the concept that the entire show is a loop that begins and ends with the murder, and subsequent un-murder, of Laura Palmer.

Lynch is credited as the Sound Designer on *Twin Peaks: The Return*, and in an interview he justified the credit, stating simply, "I'm responsible for what people see and what they hear."[22] Lynch, in many ways, treated sound as the most important element in his filmmaking; there is no question that he paid meticulous attention to the soundscapes in his work. Some of them he literally created himself: "I want to take that credit because I'm the one who makes all the final decisions on sound. In actual fact, I picked sounds and I made a few sounds."[23]

And the spinning record is an image Lynch has used before, not only in the original run of *Twin Peaks*, but also in his film *Inland Empire*. *Inland Empire* begins with a gramophone needle traveling through the groove of a record. Its path sounds endless, its sonic quality identical to the sound of the looped groove at the end of a record. We hear the same crackles and pops. It's only when we hear "Axxon N., the longest running radio play in history, tonight, continuing in the Baltic region, a grey winter day in an old hotel…" that the spell of a seemingly endless loop is broken. However, the feeling of this radio play, and the way it is incorporated throughout the film, exhibits an eternal quality—it feels like it's something that has always been here and always will be. It hums of the infinite.

The details in Lynch's work convey meaning and the details he chose to include in his films and television shows are critical to an audience's understanding of the work as a whole. It is obvious that Lynch thought long and hard about each detail he created, and in turn, his audience is compelled to think long and hard about them. When we hear the sound of a locked record groove after Cooper turns back to Laura in the woods, only to realize she's gone, the sound is played as one single revolution. As the sound stops, we are left with the sonic impression that the record has stopped spinning, or someone has lifted the stylus from the groove. This seems to telegraph the following moment when Laura disappears. Someone, presumably the director, David Lynch, has lifted her out of this groove, out of this particular storyline. As Cooper looks back, Laura's hand has disappeared from his and broken away from the salvation, and perhaps redemption, that this hand has worked the entire series up until this point to offer. The choice of using this particular sound to underscore this moment is certainly an important one. And, if that wasn't enough, Lynch goes out of his way to make sure the viewer knows the importance of this sound by having the Fireman tell Cooper—and, by proxy, the audience—in the very first episode of the third season that this sound is important to the narrative.

The first time the Firemen speaks to Cooper in the series, he says "Listen to the sounds," as he directs Cooper's attention to an old-fashioned gramophone, where a record is emitting the infinite loop of crackling and scratches. Cooper's point of view is conveyed through a moving camera as it moves toward the round horn of the device and into the dark hole at the center of it. Not only does the circular shape of the horn visually punctuate the loop of the sound, the move into its shadowy tube marks the journey into darkness that both Cooper and the viewer are about to embark upon at the start of the season.

The sound of the locked groove of a record is powerful enough on its own, insofar as metaphorically representing the cyclical nature of the show and its themes, but the fact that a vinyl record is an object that has two sides further complements Lynch's dualistic approach to his work. The sound that reverberates from a locked groove represents the end of a record, but only the *end of one side*. When the rescued Laura Palmer vanishes from the grasp of Agent Cooper at the end of Episode 17, the crackling sound of the record may indicate that while this is the end of one story, there is another parallel story spinning on the other side that features the same singer, essentially, but contains different songs and a different ending. This episode, the title of which is *The Past Dictates the Future*, ends Laura Palmer's side of the record, which is about to be flipped over to Carrie Page's side in Episode 18.

Immediately after Laura disappears in the woods, we hear her scream, but it's not just any scream; it is the same blood-curdling scream she releases in the Red Room with Agent Cooper in Episode 2 of Season 3—the same scream she emits just prior to her disappearing from that location. Lynch simply lifts the audio of that moment—the scream along with the rustling of clothes and gusts of wind—from the Red Room and places it into the scene with Cooper alone in the woods. It is an echo from the past. Or is it a reverberation from the future? "Is it future, or is it past?" Mike directed this very question to Cooper in the Red Room immediately before Laura appears in the room. Perhaps both moments are happening simultaneously, and once Laura's character is "saved" from her death, her character from the *Twin Peaks* canon disappears from every part of its storyline, including her seemingly eternal presence in the Red Room. Laura Palmer as both character and angel are no longer.

In is interesting to note that the scene in the Red Room from Season 3 Episode 2 is, itself, a replay of sorts of when we first saw Agent Cooper and Laura together in the Red Room in the first season. In other words, the sound of Laura screaming and disappearing is, essentially, an echo of an echo. Moments from the past show impact moments from the future show, and moments from the future show impact moments from the past show. The entire mechanism of *Twin Peaks* functions as an infinity loop. That is, until the moment Laura is removed from the apparatus.

The end of Episode 17 of Season 3 concludes with a performance by longtime Lynch collaborator Julee Cruise in the Bang Bang Bar. It is important to note that with the exception of James Hurley performing "Just You" and the house band playing "Audrey's Dance," Cruise's appearance is the only musical reprise from the original series to take place in this club at the end of the show. It also marks the last musical performance of Season 3, a distinction that underscores its importance.

Cruise is performing her song "The World Spins," and to understand its significance here, we must examine the first time she performs it in the original series. In what is perhaps the most earth-shattering moment in Season 2 of *Twin Peaks*, Leland Palmer is revealed as Laura Palmer's killer, namely Killer Bob. This is the moment the entire series, whether Lynch liked it or not, was leading up to: who killed Laura Palmer? In Episode 7 of this season, we hear the same sound we hear before Laura Palmer disappears from Season 3. The sound emanates from a gramophone in the Palmers' living room as a drugged and distraught Sarah Palmer crawls down her stairs toward the machine. Moments after she experiences a vision of a white horse in her living room, she loses consciousness on the floor. The camera then proceeds to track toward the spinning record and then pan to Leland Palmer looking at himself in a mirror as he adjusts his tie. Neither Sarah nor Leland stop the record; it continues to spin, and continues to emit this haunting, infinite noise.

Lynch then intercuts to The Bang Bang Bar, in which Julee Cruise is performing. As Agent Cooper watches Cruise sing "The World Spins" on stage, she transforms into the Giant (the Fireman of Season 3), who delivers a message to Cooper: "It is happening again." The image of the Giant then dissolves into a closeup of the Palmers' gramophone, its record still stuck in its groove, repeating the same crackling sound, over and over. This image is followed by Leland transforming into the face of Killer Bob in the mirror. While the unsettling sound of the needle imprisoned in its locked groove continues to reverberate, Leland brutally murders Laura's doppelganger: his niece Maddy Ferguson.

Following the murder, Lynch cuts back to Cooper watching Julee Cruise continue to sing "The World Spins." Through the technique of intercutting, Lynch ties the revelation that Leland is Bob and the murder of Maddy to Cruise performing this song. It is no coincidence that a song called "The World Spins" is directly connected to the sound of a record album spinning endlessly around a turntable. Lyrics like "The sun comes up and down each day / The river flows out to the sea" evoke the infinite. The Palmers—Leland, Sarah and, of course, Laura—are stuck in an infinite loop of abuse, a pattern that is only broken through death. Laura Palmer and her echoes, like Maddy for instance, must die. They were written to die, as there is no *Twin Peaks* without this requisite death. However, when Cooper saves Laura in Season 3, he breaks the loop within the show, as evidenced by the abrupt ending of the crackling needle sound when Laura disappears.

The show only exists if Laura dies, its ability to be played and replayed via VHS, DVD, Blu-ray and streaming services becomes impossible if she doesn't, as there is no show to write and shoot if Laura survives. Ironically, through death, Laura's character becomes immortal, crystallized inside the show known as *Twin Peaks*. Once Cooper saves her and her death is erased from the storyline, there is no story to tell and, therefore, Laura dies before she was born. She was born into death, for if she is not destined to die, there is no reason for her to be born in the first place.

In the beginning of the final episode of Season 3, Lynch replays the moment that Cooper leads Laura through the woods, toward her potential salvation, only to look back and see that she has disappeared. Following this scene, Cooper finds himself back in the Red Room, in the same scene from Episode 2. He sits across from Mike, who asks, "Is it future, or is it past?" This is not a new moment, this is the same moment from earlier in the season; however, something is noticeably different. Assuming Cooper's first-person point of view, the camera tracks toward the empty chair that Laura inhabited in the original scene. Laura is absent from this scene and, as a result of Cooper changing history, is now absent from the original scene. The loop has been broken. It is neither past nor future. It is now and now is new. *Now* is the other side of the record.

Each side of this particular record contains a world; the record spins the worlds of side A and side B. In saving Laura Palmer from her death, Cooper has lifted the stylus from the locked groove of the show—the show as we knew it—and flipped the record to the other side. Side B is familiar, the faces are the same, but the names are different and the story is not something Cooper, or the audience, have seen before. In this same Red Room sequence in the Season 3 finale, Cooper briefly remembers his meeting with Laura from Episode 2, before she quickly disappears and he encounters the Arm (it is interesting to note that Mike does not introduce it as the Evolution of the Arm this time, as he did in Episode 2), who asks him, "Is this the story of the little girl down the lane?" This is the perfect question to ask at this point, because if this story is now absent of Laura, what story is this? Who is this story about? Following this interaction, Cooper comes across Leland Palmer in the room, who tells Cooper to "Find Laura."

Laura has not disappeared from Cooper's mind, or from the mind of her deceased father/killer, or presumably from the mind of her creator, David Lynch, and these memories therefore provide the impetus to search for her. It is this impetus that drives the concluding minutes of this final episode. We may have been pulled out of the loop, but the memories of the loop remain.

WILLIAM DICKERSON

FROM TWIN PEAKS TO ODESSA, TEXAS

It wasn't until having finished watching Episode 18, the final episode of Season 3, that I understood the reworking of the opening credits, specifically, the way the waterfall is depicted on-screen. In the opening credits of the original series, Snoqualmie Falls is shot from the front at a 45-degree angle. This angle, along with the quick pan-right and tilt-down of the camera, largely obscures the fact that the waterfall is actually made up of two streams of water falling from a cliff. However, in the reimagined opening credits of Season 3, Lynch depicts the falls in an aerial shot that shoots straight down onto them. The shot begins over the two streams, a large rock between them, and then moves forward, filming the water as the two streams merge together and fall into the river below.

Every human being, in varying degrees, is divided between the capacity for good and the capacity for evil; however, we cannot sever ourselves in an effort to better examine these two sides of us. We can only undertake such a feat through artistic means, and in the case of *Twin Peaks*, Lynch accomplishes such a division through the characters of the good Cooper and the bad

Cooper. Lynch often utilized contrasting characters, people who operate as foils, in his work. The two Coopers are among the most obvious examples, but some other examples from his films include: Betty Elms and Diane Selwyn in *Mulholland Drive*, Fred Madison and Pete Dayton in *Lost Highway*, and Dorothy Valens and Sandy Williams in *Blue Velvet*. Each set of characters arguably represents two sides of an individual person.

Lynch separated his characters in this fashion as a means of underscoring the dualistic aspects and themes of his art. Keeping Lynch's approach to character separation in mind, the two streams merging into one waterfall in *Twin Peaks: The Return's* opening credits operates as the perfect visual metaphor for the final episode of the season, in which the two Coopers merge into one.

In the final episode, Lynch breaks his rules and depicts Cooper as he would be if he lived in the reality of *our* world, not the reality of *Twin Peaks*. Good Cooper's stream joins bad Cooper's stream to create one single body of water. If Episodes 1 through the first half of Episode 15 is the "real" show, and the remaining portion of Episode 15 through Episode 17 is the ersatz, or "fake," show, then Episode 18 is the "real-world" version of the show.

After Episode 18 loops back to the scene from Episode 2, in which Agent Cooper speaks with Mike in the Red Room (sans Laura Palmer's presence this time around), we witness Cooper leave the lodge the way he entered it 25 year ago: through the superimposed red curtain portal at Glastonbury Grove, an oil-filled hole surrounded by stones, located in a circle of sycamore trees in Ghostwood National Forest. It is important to note that while we see the good Cooper in the world of *Twin Peaks* throughout Season 3, it isn't until this moment that he exits the

Red Room and reenters Twin Peaks in this manner.

In Episode 3, Cooper enters the world of the show through an electrical socket. He cannot leave the Red Room and enter Twin Peaks the usual way because his doppelganger still exists in this world and, theoretically, two versions of the same person cannot exist in this world simultaneously. This assumption would seem to indicate that the portal in Glastonbury Grove remains closed to an individual until their doppelganger returns through it and trades places with them, inside the lodge. The world in which *Twin Peaks* exists can only inhabit one doppelganger at a time, which explains why the good Cooper is essentially paralyzed—both physically and mentally—when he sneaks back into it through the socket and assumes the identity of Dougie Jones. Either some part of him has been disrupted, in the molecular sense, during this journey, or the world is simply unable to properly host two versions of someone and, therefore, deference is given to the version that is already there.

As Cooper leaves the Red Room through the proper portal in Episode 18, Diane waits to greet him at Glastonbury Grove. The question of reality is front-and-center:

DIANE: *Is it you? Is it really you?*

COOPER: *(nodding) Yes. It's really me, Diane. Is it really you?*

DIANE: *Yes.*

The notion that they need to ask each other these questions, as opposed to intrinsically *knowing* the answers, underscores the limited nature of our perception—most notably, the ability to perceive, and furthermore acknowledge, both the good and bad parts of ourselves and others. It's as though the bad parts are ignorant of the good parts and the good parts are ignorant of the bad parts. This can also be said of our perception of others and our willful blindness to the intolerable parts of others: parts we end up tolerating, despite our better judgment. An excellent example of this is Sarah Palmer and her toleration of her husband's abuse of their daughter. This example is so significant that it's the engine driving the entire third season, as manifested through the metaphor of Judy and the quest to find her.

Cooper and Diane, seemingly themselves, begin driving 430 miles away from Ghostwood National Forest, the number the Fireman told Cooper to remember at the start of Season 3. As they approach the 430 mile marker—a long desert road with owl-like electrical transformers peppering the landscape—Diane asks Cooper if he is sure he wants to do this, that he doesn't "know what it's going to be like once we…" As certain as he's uncertain about what they're going to encounter, he cuts her off with assuredness, "I know that."

As they cross the threshold of 430 miles, the transformers act as a source of supernatural power, turning day to night and their expressions stoic. The shot-reverse-shot of Cooper driving and the first-person point of view of the road instantly reminds us of *Lost Highway*, and this is no coincidence. Both shots are almost identical to the shots of Fred Madison (played by Bill Pullman) who, after just transforming from Pete Dayton (played by Balthazar Getty) back to himself, is driving down a long desert road to the Lost Highway Hotel in the pitch dark, the road illuminated solely by the headlights of his car. Cooper, in this scene, is doing the exact same thing: he is driving toward a motel by the highway. The hotel, or motel, in these two Lynch works serve as the "in-between" world. In the case of *Lost Highway*, the journey to the hotel marks the transition point where Pete Dayton turns back into Fred Madison.

At this point in *Lost Highway*, we glimpse reality for the first time since the first act of the film: we see Fred's wife Renee having an affair with Dick Laurent in a seedy hotel. Until this moment, the movie had been largely internal, depicting Fred's subjective point of view of his wife's unfaithfulness and how his mind suppresses the murders of Renee and Dick Laurent. Lynch incorporates a clinical condition known as the *dissociative fugue* (formerly referred to as a *psychogenic fugue*) into the structure of the film itself. The main character Fred Madison wakes to find his wife, whom he's had a troubled relationship with, brutally murdered. After being charged with her murder and sentenced to death, he transforms into a completely different character, Pete Dayton, and starts another life in which he begins an affair with a woman who looks just like his murdered wife. Fred suffers a psychotic break, an internal reimagining of events, in which he visualizes himself as younger, more attractive and, most significantly, the one who's doing the cheating with someone else's partner rather than being cheated on by his own.

In the Lost Highway Hotel, Lynch depicts what is literally going on: Fred's wife sleeping with Laurent. We aren't just feeling it through Fred's fugue, we witness it through his physical point of view. We also witness Fred kill Laurent shortly thereafter—with the help of the Mystery Man, played by Robert Blake; this isn't realism, stylistically speaking, but we're not experiencing Fred's fugue state any longer. The hotel functions both metaphorically and literally as "the intercourse between two worlds," as the Arm might put it. In this instance, the two worlds are the realms of the subjective and objective, of surreality and reality. The hotel, or motel, is a unique location in that it is an alternate world for people: it's neither home, nor homelessness. It is transitory, like a hospital waiting area or an international airport; however, what it offers is a particular kind of privacy for those who wish to explore their shadow selves—like those in love affairs.

Just as *Lost Highway* ends its surrealistic detour and shifts back to Fred's reality at this juncture, so does *Twin Peaks: The Return*. Cooper pulls his car into a 60s style roadside motel, an establishment called The Pearblossom Motel that appears simultaneously quaint and seedy. As he exits the car, the camera remains with Diane, shooting from her perspective as she watches Cooper enter the motel office. As she gazes toward the entrance, she glimpses a different version of herself, identical in appearance, stepping out from behind the shadows of a column. Diane's expression does not change; she remains stoic, as she looks at herself. It's as though it's an apparition. Just before Cooper steps out from the office, the duplicate disappears. Its disappearance seems to telegraph the idea that this version of Diane, the version sitting in the car and about to enter the motel with Cooper, will soon cease to exist.

Inside the motel room, Cooper tells Diane to turn off the lights and approach him. As they begin to kiss, we become keenly aware of Diane's red hair and black and white fingernails, as these elements are featured in a tight close-up. Diane's hair and nails have been styled this way since she transformed from Naido to the present version of herself in Sheriff Truman's office, but these details haven't been so prominent until this moment. In behind-the-scenes footage of this sequence, Lynch instructs his cinematographer, Peter Deming, to focus specifically on Diane's fingernails: "…you see those black and white fingernails going up Kale's [sic] shoulders to his neck and his head, and working his head as you guys are going, just sort of working his head with the fingernails and fingers."[24] Is the fact that her fashion sensibilities embody the Red Room's red curtains and black and white floors merely a fan tease—an Easter egg for the audience—or is there a meaning that's more deeply tied to the narrative? I think it is safe to say that the public knew David Lynch well enough to understand that a creative decision merely for the sake of fans was an impossibility.

Diane has always been symbolic of something else. In the original series, she was personified in the form of a Dictaphone type of tape recorder, which Agent Cooper used as a method of communication with the audience. As a character seemingly unaware that there is an audience watching, Cooper cannot break the fourth wall and speak directly into the camera to us; he must use a prop from within the story as a conduit for such communication. The name of this conduit, this device, is Diane.

When Diane is finally made flesh in the form of Laura Dern in *The Return*, she turns out not to be Diane at all. In Episode 16 of Season 3, the character we think is Diane is revealed to be a *tulpa*. Tulpas are defined as entities that are created within the mind that take the form of a sentient being that may be, on the surface, indistinguishable from other sentient beings. In the case of *The Return*, tulpas are copies of preexisting individuals in the show. In a sense, they're forms of doppelgangers. If there is a distinction between these two types, the distinction may pertain to where they originate. In the world of *Twin Peaks*, doppelgangers are essentially doubles that have existed for as long as their counterparts have, whereas tulpas appear to be manufactured by their originals, or by someone else altogether. Traditionally speaking, a tulpa exists solely in the mind of the person creating it; however, this creation possesses its own will and power to think independently. The term has its roots in Tibetan Buddhism. It's curious to note that Lynch uses the term tulpa in this season in addition to the term doppelganger, which he's used before in the original series and movie. While we witness the physical manifestations of tulpas in *The Return*, if they are solely manifestations of the mind, it begs the question: whose manifestations are they? Cooper's? Lynch's? The audience's?

After the false version of Diane in *The Return* implodes and returns to the Red Room in Episode 16, where tulpas in the universe of *Twin Peaks* are created, Naido reveals herself to be seemingly hiding the real version of Diane. Naido transforms into this version of Diane in Episode 17, reuniting with Cooper in what feels like a too-good-to-be-true cliché soap opera reunion event. If it feels too-good-to-be-true, it's because it is too-good-to-be-true. Lynch peppers this character with the black, white, and red of the Red Room to make clear to the viewer that she belongs solely to the world of *Twin Peaks*, and no other world, or dimension, outside of this milieu. Indeed, all the characters in the show that is *Twin Peaks* exist solely within that world; however, Lynch seeks to make this point as clear as possible in this instance. While Naido ostensibly reveals the proper version of Diane, what is revealed is yet another tulpa. This version of Diane is not real, per se, but rather the idealized form of Diane as conjured in the mind of the dreamer.

If this is the case, then the question remains: who is the dreamer? There are numerous indications that seem to point to Special Agent Dale Cooper as being the dreamer. In Episode 17, Lynch superimposes Cooper's face in close-up over the scene in Sheriff Truman's office after Bob is destroyed. This supports the notion of him being the dreamer, as what lies beyond his face are the majority of the main cast members of the show. These characters, more or less, are representative of the entire show and we are seeing them through the filter of Cooper's face. The visual language that Lynch uses in this scene bears precedent, as he used this technique in his film *Dune* and, interestingly enough, with the same actor, Kyle MacLachlan. In *Dune*, MacLachlan plays Paul Atreides, a character that exhibits an expanded consciousness. He experiences a dream in which he realizes others want to kill him and he observes these characters in this moment through the superimposition of his face. While this particular close-up of MacLachlan is framed slightly tighter than the superimposed close-up in *The Return*, the similarity between these two moments is uncanny, and the fact that it is the same actor almost begs for the former moment to be recalled. Lynch uses the superimposition of MacLachlan's face in *Dune* to convey to the viewer that he is the dreamer dreaming the dream.

It is less clear, on its surface, that MacLachlan is dreaming during the moment of his superimposition in Episode 17 of *Twin Peaks: The Return*. However, the visual language Lynch employs, and the precedent he set when he used it *Dune*, indicates that MacLachlan, as Agent Cooper, is the dreamer dreaming the dream in Truman's office with all these characters. The most obvious indication of this is when his superimposed image states, "We live inside a dream," just before we see Cooper inside the scene speaking to the cast of characters around him and telling them, "I hope I see all of you again." And just after delivering this line, the scene cuts to a shot of David Lynch playing the character Gordon Cole. The metafictional understanding seems to be that the only way Cooper, and by proxy the audience, will be able to see all of these cast members again is if David Lynch makes it so—if he had decided to make a Season 4, let's say, for Showtime or some other network.

The conflation of the character Gordon Cole with the creator David Lynch in this moment is not an accident; it is very much intentional. The following, and final, episode of Season 3 is all about the overlap of realities, including the realities of the fictional town of Twin Peaks transitioning to the reality of *Twin Peaks* in which it exists as a show.

Lynch's use of the term tulpa, as I alluded to earlier, is an intentional shift from mental projection to literal manifestation. He could have used the term doppelganger to describe these copies of characters, but he introduced an entirely new word, and an esoteric one at that, into the lexicon of *Twin Peaks*. Given Lynch's predilection for Eastern spirituality, it is no surprise that tulpas have roots in it. Tulpas are associated with the *Trikaya* in

Tibetan Buddhism. The Trikaya is a doctrine that teaches that Buddha has three bodies: the Dharmakaya (ultimate reality), the Sambhogakaya (divine incarnation of Buddha), and the Nirmanakaya (physical incarnation of Buddha). These divided bodies are largely understood to be mental constructions, or tulpas, that originate from within the mind's eye. The splitting of a single individual into three distinct sub-entities is a concept that Lynch employs in *Twin Peaks: The Return*, specifically in regard to Agent Cooper, which makes sense if he is the dreamer. Not only do the divisions of Diane—as a tape recorder, as the evil Diane, as the idealized Red Room Diane—exist through the filter of Cooper's subjective point of view, but the three versions of himself—Good Cooper, Mr. C, and Dougie Jones—do as well.

After having crossed the 430-mile threshold and renting a room at the in-between world of the Pearblossom Motel in Episode 18, Cooper and Diane begin to have sexual intercourse. Lynch starts the scene with a reference to Episode 8, as The Platters' "My Prayer" begins to reverberate once again in the soundtrack:

And here in my heart you will stay…

The song is then cut off by Angelo Badalamenti's melancholic drone-like score, only to resume with the lyric, "My prayer," just as Diane takes her eyes off of Cooper and looks up toward the ceiling. She attempts to look at him again, kissing him, but the pain in doing so is evident. She looks up at the ceiling once again as she places her hands over Cooper's eyes, blocking his gaze. She cannot look him in the eyes, nor will she let him look at her at all.

This scene is unequivocally filmed from the point of view of Diane. For the majority of the scene, the camera remains on her side of the space, filming Cooper from over her back and shoulders; every shot of Cooper is obscured by some part of Diane's body. When Lynch films Diane's coverage, he does not match them with shots from over the back and shoulders of Cooper. Rather, he films her in a tight close-up with a frame that is unobscured, the camera positioned from above, looking down on her as though from a god's perspective. When Diane looks up toward the camera, in a state of seeming despair, the song lyrics plead:

My prayer and the answer you give,
May they still be the same for as long as we live...

If we're reading this scene literally, given our understanding of the backstory between Diane and Cooper, we may view her anguish in light of the accusation that Cooper sexually assaulted her in the past. In Episode 16, Diane's tulpa reveals in a conversation that Cooper—Mr. C's evil version of Cooper—raped her. This revelation occurs moments before she pulls a gun, is shot by the FBI, and dematerializes into thin air. The act of having sex with Cooper in the motel, no matter which version of Cooper he may be, would likely trigger memories of the past trauma she has experienced.

If we're to read this scene metaphorically, we must accept this version of Diane as the symbol she represents: the Red Room. As previously mentioned, the motel is the setting where the intercourse between two worlds occurs. Cooper enters the Pearblossom Motel at night in a world in which Twin Peaks the town exists, only to leave from a different motel, Knights Inn, the next morning in a world in which the town of Twin Peaks and the Red Room no longer exist. This point is underscored when the morning arrives and Diane is no longer there. Cooper wakes up alone. On the surface, it seems like the classic morning-after scene: a woman, whether spurned or simply hesitant to commit, abandons her lover before he wakes. However, the surface is never what the scene is about, especially in the work of David Lynch.

As Lynch films Diane from above, in what should be her moment of ecstasy, her physical expression is more aligned with grief. This makes sense. Diane, as the stand-in for the Red Room, is mourning Agent Cooper's departure from its world, a world that is, essentially, mourning the loss of its main character. Cooper is crossing over into a realm in which the Red Room does not exist, which explains why Diane disappears the next morning, after the intercourse between two worlds is complete. Neither Diane nor the Red Room exist here. In the note she left Cooper, whom she now refers to as Richard, she writes, "I don't recognize you anymore. I'm sorry, whatever it was we had together is over." The Red Room doesn't recognize him anymore, either, as he has entered a place where the Red Room is "non-exist-ent." He has left the confines of our television sets, in which the show and its characters exist, and has entered the world in which we, the audience, exist and *Twin Peaks* is just a television program.

The Dear Richard note, Lynch's take on the Dear John letter, seems to confuse Cooper. After he reads the signature on the note, Linda, he repeats the two names, "Richard" and "Linda," uttering them with abject bewilderment. This is unusual for Cooper, considering the Fireman specifically told Cooper to remember the names Richard and Linda. These two names were of great importance to Cooper. Therefore, it seems as though he has forgotten to remember them, that crossing over to this other world has resulted in him forgetting details of his recent past. While some may read into the origins of these names, looking for clues (for instance, some believe there is a connection to Richard Horne, the son of Audrey and Mr. C), I tend to think that the pedestrian nature of the names is the point. They're the types of names you forget, and that's exactly what Cooper does—he forgets them.

When Cooper leaves the motel in the morning, it becomes clear that it is not the same motel he checked into the night before. While Lynch shot the night scenes at the Pearblossom Motel, he shot the morning scenes at the Knights Inn in Palmdale, California. In contrast to the Pearblossom Motel's retro aesthetic, the Knights Inn exhibits a more modern, if not similarly rundown, look. The shift from past to future is also highlighted by the 1963 Ford 300 car that Cooper drives to the motel, which transforms into the 2003 Lincoln Town Car that he finds parked outside of his motel in the morning.

The next morning, when we see Agent Cooper leave his motel room, in a distinctly different location, he walks without hesitation to a distinctly different car—the Lincoln—as though it is, indeed, his car. He takes a moment to look at the car and back at the hotel, but this look is more indicative of forgetting what was, rather than not knowing what is. His hair, while combed neatly, is without its signature gel; his trademark coif is missing. It's as though he just stepped out of the shower, gave it a quick comb, then left the room—in other words, how most ordinary men tend to their hair in the morning. While this detail may seem trivial, it corresponds with Lynch's ultimate point: the Cooper we are presented with here is not the Cooper of the fictional world of *Twin Peaks* any longer; he is the Cooper as living, breathing human being, existing now in this same reality in which we live. Or maybe it's just a continuity error.

Prior to Cooper crossing over to this new dimension, Lynch presented him as separate people, which is perhaps reflective of the three bodies of the Buddhist Trikaya (though, it can be argued that Dougie, if he is to count as a third manifestation of Cooper, is simply the good Cooper, only paralyzed). In reality, human beings cannot be divided into separate entities—we are all those entities wrapped up into one being. The Cooper of the series—the good Cooper—is the character the audience knows and loves, and that character is perfect. Lynch shows Cooper's imperfections through the divided selves of Mr. C and, to an extent, Dougie. But the character we are presented with now is someone who is not perfect, and Lynch begins to hint not only at these imperfections, but also at the fact that what was once divided has now become whole. It is no coincidence that the 2003 Lincoln Town Car is the same model car—and, in all likelihood, the same exact vehicle—that Mr. C drives earlier in the season. While Lynch forgoes Mr. C's long hair in favor of short hair that is slightly disheveled, he makes Cooper's connection to Mr. C clearer with the choice to have Cooper drive Mr. C's car. The inference seems to be that Mr. C is now a part of the good Cooper in totality, and this becomes even more apparent in the later scenes.

The two streams of water at the peak of Snoqualmie Falls have joined together as it pours into the river below. The promise of this metaphorical premise in the opening credit sequence has finally been fulfilled.

Shortly after Cooper drives out of the motel parking lot, Lynch cuts to a shot of a sign for the Odessa, Texas city limit, population 99,940. This immediately calls to mind the population sign for the town of Twin Peaks in the title sequence for the original series, an image that is etched into the minds of all *Twin Peaks* fans. The shot of the Odessa sign is an important shot for several reasons. Like the shot of the Twin Peaks sign, it marks the beginning of a sequence: in the case of the original series, it marked the beginning of an episode, and in a sense, the shot of the Odessa sign marks the beginning of an episode as well. This moment in Episode 18 officially demarcates the beginning of Cooper's journey through the new dimension of the show, the dimension he crossed into a few scenes earlier. Once Cooper arrives in Odessa, the show previously known as *Twin Peaks* becomes something entirely different.

As mentioned in an earlier chapter, co-writer Mark Frost said that *Twin Peaks: The Return* is modeled after Homer's *Odyssey* and the choice of town name seems to support that notion. At first blush, the concept of returning home seems to apply to Cooper leaving the confines of the Red Room in which he's been trapped for 25 years—similar to Odysseus trapped on Calypso's

island—and returning to Twin Peaks. This idea is the most obvious correlation to the *Odyssey*; however, there are numerous echoes, another being its use of godlike characters. Like Athena being born from Zeus' head, Laura Palmer springs from the Fireman's head, conjuring her as a force of good from his own version of Mount Olympus: his castle on the purple sea. It is Athena who persuades Zeus to send Hermes to help Odysseus escape from Calypso's clutches. In a reflection of this myth, it is only after Cooper asks Laura when he can leave the Red Room in Season 3, Episode 2 that she kisses him and Mike, the series' Hermes-like character, assists in his escape and facilitates his journey back to Twin Peaks. In Episode 18, however, the concept of *returning* implies something different: a return from fiction back to the reality in which the fiction was created.

The universe of *Twin Peaks* relies heavily on fictionalized places, businesses, and organizations. There is the town of Twin Peaks, of course, as well as examples like the Double R Diner, Ghostwood National Forest, the Great Northern, Big Ed's Gas Farm, Buckhorn, Rancho Rosa Estates, and the Silver Mustang Casino, among many others. However, the fictionalization of such locations and entities ends when Cooper arrives in Odessa. David Lynch has always relied on imagined locales to help deepen the mystery of the settings in which his stories take place, therefore when confronted with the stark reality of places in Episode 18, we're naturally thrown off balance.

As Cooper drives through Odessa, we glimpse fragments from our reality, such as the Maersk shipping containers prominently featured in the background. These containers surround a diner called Eat At Judy's, which draws Cooper's attention and prompts him to pull into its parking a lot.

In my research, I discovered that Eat At Judy's does not exist; however, it's about as close to real as it can possibly get. The production shot on location at a restaurant called Eat At Rudy's in Wilmington, California and simply replaced the "R" on the sign with a "J." There is no shortage of diners in California, where Eat At Rudy's resides, or Texas, where Eat At Judy's supposedly resides. Lynch could have chosen any diner and simply dressed it the way he wanted, or he could have built a diner on a soundstage per the specifications in his head. However, it seems as though the production's locations department went out of its way to find an existing diner called Judy's. My speculation is that Eat At Rudy's was the closest diner that Lynch and company could find that fit the bill, otherwise, they would have shot at an establishment with "Judy" in its title.

The adherence to our—the audience's—reality in the final half of Episode 18, as opposed to the fictional reality of *Twin Peaks* prior to the shift to Odessa, is of utmost importance to the narrative. It's interesting to note that the Pearblossom Motel, while once a working establishment, in recent years has been operating solely as a filmmaking location for movies and television. This location stands in contrast to the working, and quite real, Knight's Inn, that Cooper wakes up in, bidding good morning to his new reality, a reality in which fiction no longer exists.

Inside Eat At Judy's, we are presented with a scene we've seen nearly countless times before in this show: Cooper sitting down in a diner booth and ordering coffee. However, this time, his behavior is noticeably different. He is visibly stoic and humorless, nodding in response to the waitress's question about coffee and then asking in a monotone if another waitress works there. She confirms there is another waitress, but that it's her day off. At this point in the episode, it becomes clear that Cooper is looking for someone, but it is unclear who that someone is. As he sips his coffee, it is quite obvious that this is not the same Cooper we know from the series. With the exception of the coffee Pete Martell brewed for him with a fish in the percolator, Cooper never had a bad cup of coffee. His reactions after drinking a cup would be an ear-to-ear smile along with a superlative of some kind like the famous, "that's a damn fine cup of coffee." In Eat At Judy's, he might as well be sipping plain hot water, as his reaction is expressionless. In this world, coffee no longer holds the same pleasure, or meaning, for him as it once did.

Lynch could not be providing the audience with a bigger clue that Cooper is no longer the same Cooper. And in the following moments, we realize this new Cooper is a version of himself that has become integrated with Mr. C. As he sits in his booth, sipping his coffee, he witnesses a group of cowboys a few booths down disrespecting and groping the waitress who just served him. Cooper, both matter-of-factly and classically chivalrous, tells them to "leave her alone." Predictably, the cowboys do not take kindly to his interjection and they get up and bring their collective intimidation over to him. Cooper's nonchalant attitude, defiantly leaning back and placing an arm around the seat behind him, is more akin to Mr. C's cocky bravado. Rather than de-escalate the situation, Cooper seems to be inviting, almost daring, these men to make the first move. As one of the men pulls a firearm and aims it at Cooper, what ensues is indicative of the perfect amalgamation of Coopers, both good and bad. Cold, methodical, machinelike, Cooper neutralizes the threat in no time at all. It's as though the Mr. C we saw dispatch the man with the rifle when picking up Ray and Daria earlier in the season has merged with the Dougie Jones we saw spring into action to defend himself against Ike "The Spike's" assassination attempt.

After disarming the cowboys, Cooper proceeds to survey the rest of the restaurant, pointing his gun at everyone as he does so. This Cooper trusts no one. After ordering the waitress to write the address of the missing waitress on a piece of paper, he then, somewhat recklessly, places the cowboys' guns into the boiling oil of a deep fryer. The decision to destroy the weapons is the responsible thing to do; however, the way in which he goes about doing so borders on the irresponsible, as he warns the cook that the bullets may go off. This appears to be the action of Agent Cooper who is acting both as the good Cooper and Mr. C.

The notion that Cooper is no longer divided, that he is the sum of his fictionalized parts, is further accentuated when he visits the home of Carrie Page.

As Carrie, played by Sheryl Lee, opens the door to Cooper, he is visibly stunned. If he was looking for Judy, he did not find her. His stoic behavior and monotone delivery immediately soften as the sight of her engenders a clear sense of empathy. This is a noticeable shift in attitude from the previous scene in the diner. He becomes even more baffled when he asks her if she is Laura Palmer and she has no idea what he is talking about, responding almost too emphatically, that her name is "Carrie Page." While

Cooper may have forgotten elements of his life prior to crossing over, he most certainly hasn't forgotten Laura Palmer or his mission to save her. Though, it seems Carrie Page has. Despite her denials, Cooper insists that he believes her to be Laura Palmer and that it's important that he bring her back to her home in Twin Peaks, Washington. The only crack in her armor, per se, is when Cooper mentions her mother's name, Sarah. Carrie's reaction is a mixture of bewilderment and fright when Sarah's name is mentioned, which is not unlike the audience's reaction, assumably, at this point in the episode.

It is at this point that I am reminded again of *Lost Highway*, specifically the film's implication that its main character experiences a dissociative fugue. However, there is a distinct difference. In *Lost Highway*, Fred Madison's fugue state is treated subjectively—he starts a new life inside his mind while in jail, therefore Lynch depicts him physically as someone else living a different life outside of prison. In reality, Fred never leaves his jail cell. However, in Episode 18 of *Twin Peaks: The Return*, Laura Palmer's fugue state is treated objectively; her state reflects the literal interpretation of a *dissociative fugue*, a state common in persons with dissociative identity disorder, as described by the Diagnostic and Statistical Manual of Mental Disorders, also known as DSM-5.[25] There is no different actor, no surrealistic style, no signature Angelo Badalamenti score. In essence, after Cooper crosses over and meets Carrie Page, Lynch strips his material of David Lynch. Lynch was always interested in depicting the real-world repercussions of trauma on his characters, but he was never interested in portraying them in a realistic manner. He uses metaphor and dream logic as techniques in his work to make the audience feel what his characters are feeling, because feelings are subjective.

But in real life, when dealing with traumas other people experience, we do not have art—in this case, filmmaking—to get inside others' thoughts and feelings; we simply have the surface reality that we observe from which to work.

In the majority of *Twin Peaks*, Laura Palmer's life is depicted through the lens of her subjective emotions, and the technique Lynch uses is the metaphor of demons, specifically Bob and Judy as her persecutors, as opposed to conveying the objective reality, in which the persecutors are her parents. In reality, which is what Lynch is depicting in the second half of Episode 18, there is no metaphor; we are being presented with the real-world ramifications of the trauma that was inflicted upon Laura and her life choices since she endured this trauma.

In television, there needs to be a murder. *Who killed Laura Palmer* is the question that not only started a show, but a phenomenon; however, in reality, trauma for individuals rarely ends in such soap opera fashion. Trauma persists, plaguing an individual year after year as they grow older, and if Laura Palmer had been a real person, and had not died, she would perhaps turn out to be someone like Carrie Page.

David Lynch rarely explained his work and any time he came close to doing so, it was either purposefully vague or an accident. When speaking publicly about *Lost Highway*, whether intentionally or not, he seemed to have explained more than any other film or show he's worked on, and his explanations are tied directly to the concept of the dissociative, or psychogenic, fugue. In his book, *Catching the Big Fish*, Lynch writes in regard to the film: "What struck me about O.J. Simpson was that he was able to smile and laugh. He was able to go golfing with seemingly very few problems about the whole thing. I wondered how, if a person did these deeds, he could go on living. And we found this great psychology term—'psychogenic fugue'—describing an event where the mind tricks itself to escape some horror. So, in a way, *Lost Highway* is about that. And the fact that nothing can stay hidden forever."[26]

In an interview with *Filmmaker Magazine* at the time of the film's release, Lynch went into more detail:

> **LYNCH:** *Sometime during the shooting, the unit publicist was reading up on different types of mental illness, and she hit upon this thing called "psychogenic fugue." The person suffering from it creates in their mind a completely new identity, new friends, new home, new everything—they forget their past identity. This has reverberations with Lost Highway, and it's also a music term. A fugue starts off one way, takes up on another direction, and then comes back to the original, so it [relates] to the form of the film.*
>
> **FILMMAKER:** *There are psychological pressures at work on the different characters in Lost Highway, and I guess what the audience might identify with is the acting out of certain repressed desires. But the story unfolds on a supernatural level at the same time...*
>
> **LYNCH:** *Well, sometimes, mental things could appear that way outside the condition.*
>
> **FILMMAKER:** *Can you expand on that?*
>
> **LYNCH:** *No.*[27]

This is a fascinating interview in which Lynch connects the story and structure of his film to a documented disorder. To say this was unlike David Lynch is an understatement, as he has repeatedly expressed over the years, his preference for allowing the audience to interpret his films themselves, rather than him interpreting his films for them. He also addresses the notion of metaphor in his work, equating the "supernatural" elements with a projection of someone's mental state. He is speaking to this in regard to *Lost Highway*, but such a statement also applies to *Twin Peaks*, specifically to his use of such supernatural elements as Bob and Judy as external projections of his characters' mental states.

The co-writer of *Lost Highway*, Barry Gifford, has said in regard to the film, "What if one person woke up one day and was another person? We had to create a scenario to make that plausible. We discovered a clinical, psychological condition which fit our premise—a 'psychogenic fugue.' It's as if you decided to change your life and showed up with a different name and entirely created a new identity for yourself and really grew to believe you were this new person."[28] This fugue state occurs inside the head of Fred Madison, and Lynch films the inside of his head, visually externalizing the character's inward journey in the movie, otherwise all he would be able to do was simply film a man sitting inside a jail cell. Gifford confirmed this fact in another interview: "In Fred Madison's case, he's going mad anyway especially with the inability to control his wife and being thrown in prison where he can't flee. He's on death row, so he experiences a fugue which is entirely within his own mind, so what we're seeing is his fantasy."[29] With respect to *Twin Peaks: The Return*, however, Laura Palmer experiences a fugue state in which she assumes a new identity and physically starts a new life elsewhere, and that's exactly what Lynch films.

Dissociative fugues often occur in people with dissociative identity disorders, which is precisely what Laura Palmer suffers from. Laura finds it impossible to reconcile that her father is her rapist and, as a result, creates Bob as a means of separating the good part of her father from the bad. She simply cannot comprehend the reality of the abuse and this type of mental dissociation helps protect her from further psychological harm. According to the DSM-5, dissociative identity disorder is associated with overwhelming experiences, traumatic events, and/or abuse occurring in childhood. Laura's childhood is marred with sexual abuse at the hands of her father and at the hands of older men in her community.

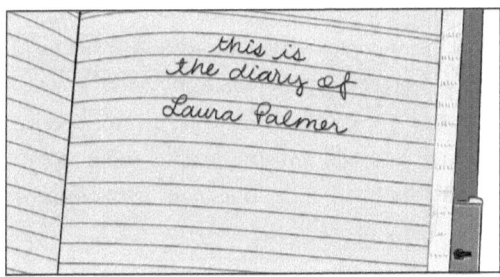

The Secret Diary of Laura Palmer, the best-selling book written by David Lynch's daughter Jennifer, and an official part of the *Twin Peaks* canon, reads as a textbook example of a person suffering from dissociative identity disorder. Not only does the book provide numerous accounts of statutory rape— Laura, from the ages of 13 to 16, engaging in sexual contact with older men—and alludes to her abusive encounters with Bob—i.e., her father—but it also presents Laura as someone who is split into two different personas:

> *Sometimes I think there is someone inside me, but it is another, stranger part of me. Sometimes I see her in the mirror. I don't know that I ever want to have children of my own. Something happens to parents, or people who become parents. I think they forget they were ever children themselves and that things might embarrass or upset their kids sometimes, but they have just forgotten or decided to ignore that. Too many bad things happen to me sometimes late at night, so I probably would not be such a good mother. This makes me sad inside.*[30]

This excerpt, dated August 31, 1984, is written from the perspective of someone just barely a teenager. This is a child that has been sexually abused, but at the time of the abuse, she could not fully comprehend the gravity of the actions being perpetrated against her, nor could she articulate who is to blame. She links her parents to her being psychologically split; however, as the years progress, she also splits who is to blame. Specifically, she splits her father into two separate people: the good person Leland/Dad, and the bad person Bob. This is the only way she is able to go on living her life:

> *I wonder if Mom has ever felt anything that I'm feeling…? I sense that some of my experiences are ones that she would understand, but she comes from a family and a generation that doesn't really like to talk about things that make them uncomfortable. Maybe BOB makes her feel uncomfortable. Maybe Dad knows BOB, too, but Mom won't let us talk about him because it makes everyone…so upset…? I don't know.*[31]

This diary entry seems to not only imply that Laura believes her father to be connected to Bob in some fashion, but also that her mother is aware of Bob and his connection to her father. Simply stated, it seems as though Leland's sexual abuse of his daughter is known to everyone in the house. It is a corruption at the heart of the Palmer household and the house rule is not to address it. They just don't talk about it. It's the unspoken reality of their lives that is too painful to confront, for to confront it would shatter the idealized version of their existence. Laura splits herself and her parents in order to cope with the trauma she has endured and will continue to endure: "I know I can control this. I know I can *SEE BOB BECAUSE HE IS REAL. A REAL THREAT. TO YOU, LAURA PALMER,*" she writes to herself, in the third person. "*TO EVERYONE AROUND YOU.*"[32]

The first two seasons of *Twin Peaks* focus on the repercussions of Leland's abuse, and subsequent murder, of his daughter. The movie *Fire Walk with Me* focuses on Laura's ultimate acceptance of the reality of the abuse. However, her mother's denial, and ostensible cover-up, of this abuse is what *Twin Peaks: The Return* focuses on in its search for the enigmatic Judy. When Cooper tells Carrie Page that her parents' names are Leland and Sarah, she is visibly confused, but also noticeably upset, when she hears "Sarah." We understand from the series, film, and *The Secret Diary of Laura Palmer* that "Bob" is Laura's name for the bad part of her father, but what if "Judy" was her name for the bad part of her mother? What if Laura had read the children's book *Bob and Judy* when she was younger and borrowed those names to split her parents' identities? What if she simply used her mother's middle name, "Judith," to dissociate the loving part of her mother from the corrupt part?

Those who suffer from dissociative identity disorder in their youth often develop other symptoms as they grow older. According to the DSM-5, "Dissociation in children may generate problems with memory, concentration, attachment, and traumatic play. Nevertheless, children usually do not present with identity changes."[33] However, older individuals may experience "cognitive disorders due to dissociative amnesia."[34] The DSM-5 further clarifies dissociative amnesia as "an inability to recall autobiographical information that is inconsistent with normal forgetting. It may or may not involve purposeful travel or bewildered wandering (i.e., fugue)."[35]

With respect to Laura Palmer and her assuming the identity of Carrie Page in Episode 18, her dissociative amnesia correlates to the DSM-5's definition. In *Fire Walk with Me*, Laura allowed herself to be killed rather than possessed by Bob, which ended the cycle of abuse and resulted in the restoration of her spirit in the Red Room. In *Twin Peaks: The Return*, Cooper diverted her from this ending, and in doing so, forced her to continue to deal with the trauma she endured in her life. The method through which her mind continues to deal with the trauma is to increase the severity of her dissociative identity disorder by entering a fugue state, and it is Laura in this fugue state that Cooper meets in Odessa, Texas.

IS IT FUTURE OR IS IT PAST?

If Agent Cooper had told Carrie Page that the names of her parents were Bob and Judy, instead of Leland and Sarah, would she have recognized them? Would she have acknowledged them as her parents? Or have those names been repressed alongside the names Leland and Sarah, and mostly everything else from her teenage years?

These are important questions to ask, but they don't necessarily need to be answered. Carrie's response to the mention of Sarah's name clues both the audience and Cooper to the notion that Laura Palmer, in some fashion, is a part of Carrie Page. In addition, the fact that she allows an FBI agent into her house when a dead man sits in her living room is another clue that she is not only freely able to dissociate from traumatic events or circumstances, but also still drawn—willingly or unwillingly—to such traumatic events or circumstances. In regard to the mental condition at the heart of *Lost Highway*, Barry Gifford has said, "This fugue state allows [Fred Madison] to create a fantasy world, but within this fantasy world, the same problems occur."[36] In *Twin Peaks: The Return*, while Laura has physically created a second life, replete with a new name and fresh location, she is destined to endure similar traumas and repeat the same mistakes that plagued her first life.

The idea that Laura has been saved from one life of traumas only to endure another life of traumas is something that Cooper must grapple with, and it is this grappling that he struggles with from the moment he meets Carrie Page until the end of the series. In his role of playing God, if you will, he was able to control one outcome but, tragically, not all outcomes. Cooper made the decision to rewrite the history of Laura's life, and consequently the history of the show, while he was the good Cooper, the idealistic version of himself. If Cooper had been his whole self, as he is after he crosses over in Episode 18, he might have foreseen the problems Laura encounters, but his idealism blinded him.

Lynch touches on something akin to the feeling of regret as Cooper reconnects with Laura as Carrie Page. Lynch intends for the audience to question Cooper's decision to save Laura because idealism, in its most extreme sense, comes with a set of blinders, and Special Agent Dale Cooper embodies idealism in its most extreme sense. The good Cooper's optimism, when not counterbalanced with Mr. C's pessimism, can be detrimental to both himself and those around him, because life is not separated into black and white parts, or good and evil. Life is an amalgamation of both, and to ignore one side in favor of the other is a mistake. This is entirely Lynch's point and it sums up the theme of *Twin Peaks* and most of his body of work.

As Cooper enters Page's home, he is taken aback by the dead body of a man in her loveseat. He's been shot through the head, his arms protruding outward, the result of rigor mortis. It's clear the corpse has been there for a while and Carrie's ignoring it in the presence of a stranger—a stranger with a badge, no less—speaks to her denial of the situation, the type of denial that's clearly abnormal and likely indicative of mental instability. However, what is more shocking is the fact that Cooper actively denies the situation, too. He reacts to the dead man, and is visibly affected by it emotionally, but he makes the choice not to investigate further.

This choice is simply antithetical to who Agent Cooper is, at least the Agent Cooper we know from the television series up until this point. To ignore a crime, and furthermore, to ignore the criminal—assuming Carrie is responsible for the murder of this man—is unfathomable for the good Cooper. Not only to ignore the criminal, but to aid the criminal's escape: these actions are more in line with Mr. C's character and choices he would make.

After Cooper looks twice at the man, his eyes exhibiting a tangible sense of horror, he turns to the statuette of a white horse displayed atop Carrie's mantel. As I explored earlier, the white horse as product of rape is a characteristic that is shared with the white horse in Sarah's vision, as the white horse appears when Leland is raping, or preparing to rape, Laura. Lynch has firmly established the white horse as a symbol of abuse and murder, specifically toward Laura (the exception being its appearance just prior to the murder of Maddy; however, Maddy acts as a proxy for Laura), and that association must be considered as Cooper stares at the statuette. As he looks at it, his expression changes. His expression transitions from shock to a semblance of understanding. Why has this man been killed? Perhaps Lynch provides us with the answer in the form of the white horse statuette: he abused Carrie/Laura.

If Cooper infers this from his glance at the statuette, and the result is Carrie/Laura killing her abuser, he might have used this rationale as justification to *look the other way*. This moment directly contrasts with the scene in which the white horse appears to Cooper in the Red Room in Episode 2 of Season 3. Unlike Sarah Palmer, who focuses directly on the horse when it appears to her, Cooper's attention moves past the horse and settles on the darkness around it. This operates as a visual metaphor highlighting Lynch's theme. Instead of looking at the white horse, like Sarah, Cooper chooses the opposite of turning away from the darkness: he heads toward it.

The concept of not looking at evil directly is exactly what Lynch's theme of balance opposes. His theme reflects the idea that one must look at evil in order to be good, to achieve good and be capable of goodness. In other words, good people don't divert their eyes from evil; they confront it.

In Carrie Page's home, Cooper chooses to turn away from the darkness—i.e., the dead man and the ramifications of his murder—and look at the horse. Lynch cuts to a shot of the living room from over Cooper's left shoulder. The white horse is framed on the left, on the same side as the camera, and the dead man is framed on the right. Cooper is presented with a choice here, as suggested through Lynch's visual grammar: to focus on the dead man, and in doing so, address the problem, or focus on the white horse, and in doing so, ignore the problem. The fact that the camera weighs toward the side of the horse telegraphs his decision: he ignores the dead man and helps Carrie escape the scene of a presumable crime.

Cooper, an agent of the law, should arrest her, or at least report this scene to the local authorities, but he decides to literally, and metaphorically, look the other way. He is too focused on his obsession, which manifests in selfishness, with respect to saving Laura Palmer. In this moment, Cooper has committed a sin, the same sin that Sarah Palmer committed, only less severe. The fact that he is guilty of committing such a sin is evidence that the Cooper we are now witnessing on-screen is Cooper as a human being in whole form, and therefore, flawed.

Once Cooper decides not to address the dead man in the room, he doesn't look over at him again. He completely ignores him, keeping his eyes on Carrie/Laura as she reenters the room. It is important to keep in mind that what Cooper is seeing before him is a direct result of the actions he took when he decided to alter the trajectory of Laura's life and, as a result, the history inside the show itself.

Cooper's decision, and its consequences, directly relates to the Tao and the concepts of the yin and yang, wherein every action creates a counteraction. Similar to the Hindu concept of Karma, these counteractions are inevitable and must be accepted as such. It is through this acceptance that one can operate within the flow of natural existence and live a productive and fruitful life. Cooper must come to grips with the results of his decision and how it has affected not only the life of Laura Palmer/Carrie Page, but also others, including the dead man in her living room. However, he's not ready to accept the reality of the situation, as he proceeds to pluck Carrie/Laura from her problem life and take her home.

As they begin to drive out of town, toward the town of Twin Peaks, Washington, the concept of reality is immediately brought to the forefront. Carrie Page asks Cooper, "Are you really an FBI Agent?" He reassures her that he is as he shows her his badge. This is the perfect question to ask as we witness the characters in this show transition from a fictional world with a specific set of rules to a world aligned with our reality.

As they continue to drive, Lynch dissolves the scene, shifting from day to a dark night out on the road. In what at first glance seems benign, a pair of headlights appears behind them for an extended period of time, prompting Carrie to ask if they're being followed. Lynch films this scene rather conventionally, employing a medium two-shot and single close-ups on his characters, all while keeping the headlights present in the background. The outlier in this sequence is a profile shot of Carrie from outside the passenger side of the car. Shortly after she asks Cooper if they're being followed, Lynch cuts to this shot wherein Carrie is positioned at the extreme right of the frame. Her eye-line is left to right as she looks out the front windshield, the empty backseat and rear windshield illuminated by the headlights, which consume the rest of the frame behind her. The attention Lynch pays to the space behind Carrie—Carrie, specifically, as Lynch does not match this shot with a similar shot of Cooper from the other side—is significant, and the concept of lights following her, illuminating that space, places more emphasis on the space than the character.

The meaning of this sequence of shots seems clear: Carrie and, by extension, Cooper cannot escape the ramifications of their actions. The consequences will follow them. The natural order of the Tao is grounded in balance, and with every pendulum swing of action comes a resulting swing of counteraction. It's impossible to run—or in this case, drive—away from the path of that swing.

Carrie begins to open up further to Cooper and hint that she is aware of her past life, as she remarks that she had tried to keep a "clean house" in Odessa, perhaps implying that she had not kept a clean house prior to that. She goes on to say, "In those days, I was too young to know any better." There has been no mention of any other part of Carrie's life aside from Cooper sharing his thoughts that he believes her to be Laura Palmer; therefore, it stands to reason that it is Laura Palmer's life she is referring to here. It feels like an admission of sorts, confirming Cooper's suspicions, suspicions she was not ready, or able, to confirm earlier when they met at her door.

They stop at a Valero gas station, a decidedly different repository of gas than Big Ed's Gas Farm, to say the least, and further evidence that they are indeed traversing the audience's reality as opposed to the reality of the show. Lynch continues to document their journey with little to no stylistic subjectivity. He incorporates numerous dissolves to show the passage of time, but other than that common editorial technique, this sequence lacks Lynch's expressionistic filmmaking. For Lynch, who is credited as the sound designer, to leave the soundtrack void of music, drones, or sound effects draws our attention to the fact that there are no music, drones, or sound effects accompanying this journey. Lynch wants us to notice the silence, to become aware of the objective reality of the sound, of the locations, of this non-*Twin Peaks* atmosphere. This awareness practically leads to cognitive dissonance when Cooper drives past the Mar-T Double R Diner, as the real Mar-T Cafe—currently known as Twede's Cafe—was used to shoot all the Double R Diner scenes in Season 3, along with its scenes in the show's pilot and the movie *Fire Walk with Me*. This location is largely the same in both the fictional world of *Twin Peaks* and the nonfictional world outside of the show.

Initially, Lynch wants us to believe the diner that Cooper is passing is the fictional diner, as Cooper himself believes he is driving through Twin Peaks, but of course, there's nothing fictional about the diner, or the town, to him. It is only after the episode concludes that we are left along with Cooper to reevaluate our entire perception of the town we thought was Twin Peaks, as it doesn't seem like the Twin Peaks we know at all—it seems much more like the town of North Bend, Washington where *Twin Peaks* was shot.

As they continue to drive through the residential section of this area, Cooper asks Carrie if she recognizes anything, to which she responds, "No." Cooper eventually pulls to the side of the road outside a white house with the number 708. The house is, unmistakably, the same house that is home to the Palmers in *Twin Peaks*. When Cooper asks her if she recognizes the house, she responds, "No." The first time we—the audience—see the house is when Carrie looks at it and we see it through her point of view. The choice to withhold showing the viewer the house until Carrie looks at it is significant. Lynch crafts a moment that perfectly exemplifies cognitive dissonance: the viewer recognizes the house through the eyes of the person whose house it is; however, she, herself, does not recognize it. By way of the viewer, Lynch conveys the idea that part of this person does, indeed, recognize the house.

Both Cooper and Carrie step out of the car and approach the home. In a series of two-shots, close-ups and reverse-shots of the house, we are party to every single step they take as they ascend toward the front door. Lynch continues to keep his soundtrack clear of anything but the natural noises of the night in order to keep the audience grounded in the real-time of this moment. After Cooper knocks on the door, a woman he does not recognize answers, and he introduces himself as an FBI agent. He then proceeds to ask her questions about Sarah Palmer. This woman has never heard of Sarah Palmer and tells Cooper that she is the person who owns the house. Cooper continues to question her about the house and discovers that she bought the house from someone named, "Mrs. Chalfont," and that her name is, "Alice Tremond."

In what seems like a scene devoid of anything having to do with *Twin Peaks*, these names function as echoes of the show. There is a Mrs. Tremond in the original series of *Twin Peaks*, and the actor who plays that role also plays the role of Mrs. Chalfont in *Fire Walk with Me*. This character is, essentially, the same character; she simply changes names from one medium to the other. In the screenplay for *Fire Walk with Me*, while other characters refer to her as Mrs. Chalfont, the character descriptions still refer to her as Mrs. Tremond. In Episode 9 of Season 2, when Donna Hayward, played by Lara Flynn Boyle, brings Agent Cooper to see Mrs. Tremond to question her about Harold Smith's death, another woman answers the door of her home. This other woman claims to be Mrs. Tremond, but she is not the same Mrs. Tremond whom Donna had met before. In fact, she claims to be the only Mrs. Tremond there; she knows of no other Mrs. Tremond, related or otherwise.

The previous time Donna met Mrs. Tremond was when she delivered her Meals on Wheels. When she made the visit, she encountered an older woman and her grandson, and the apartment looked completely different from the apartment she visits later with Cooper.

In *Fire Walk with Me*, Mrs. Tremond appears as one of the entities in the Room Above the Convenience Store, alongside her grandson, the Arm, Bob, the Jumping Man, and various Woodsmen. This scene is superimposed over the scene of Phillip Jeffries, played by David Bowie, returning to FBI Headquarters after a long, unanticipated absence, stating emphatically as he enters, "I'm not gonna talk about Judy; in fact, we're not gonna talk about Judy at all." Both scenes begin by dissolving in and out of each other, as though they are two competing realities, before the convenience store scene takes precedence. The scene with Phillip Jeffries, essentially, becomes a voice-over track, informing what we are seeing in the room above the store. As we hear Jeffries say the line, "We live inside a dream," Lynch cuts to Mrs. Tremond and her grandson sitting in the room.

Lynch uses the motif of television static as a transitional device to connect both of these scenes together. This motif underscores the metafictional facets of the film. The dream that Phillip Jeffries claims they are living in is the world of fiction. They are characters from a television show—that is the world within which they exist and not only are the occupants in the Room Above the Convenience Store aware of this, they are also somehow a conduit to the other side: the other side being our reality in which the television show is broadcast. Visually, it's as though someone—perhaps *the dreamer*—is adjusting an antenna to get a better signal, generating the static as the two channels fade in and out of each other.

In 2014, Lynch uncharacteristically released a series of deleted scenes from *Fire Walk with Me*, calling them *The Missing Pieces*. Lynch, someone who refused to include chapter stops on his DVDs and Blu-rays, was not usually one to indulge extra material outside his work, as he intended the work to stand on its own. He even hosted a premiere of *The Missing Pieces*, a premiere I was lucky to be able to attend, at the Vista Theater in Los Angeles. The release of this bonus material, and Lynch's collaboration in its release, serve to officially validate the work as part of the *Twin Peaks* canon. These are not just deleted scenes; these are *The Missing Pieces*.

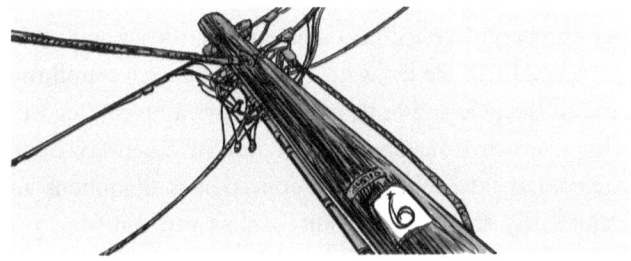

In *Fire Walk with Me*, the scene above the convenience store is truncated, having been shortened in length for the feature release time. However, the scene was released in its entirety as part of *The Missing Pieces*. In the unedited sequence, the Arm speaks to the entities around him, saying the following: "From pure air. We have descended... from pure air. Going up and down. Intercourse between the two worlds." When he says the words, "We have descended," Lynch cuts to Mrs. Tremond and her grandson—the inference being that the Tremonds, along with the others sitting around them, have descended from pure air. The key to understanding these lines is the first shot of the sequence. Lynch begins the scene with a shot of power lines, which slowly tilts down to a large number 6 accompanied by smaller numbers reading 324810 on the utility pole. This particular pole is situated at the Fat Trout Trailer Park. This is the pole that Agent Chet Desmond, played by Chris Isaak, sees just before he finds Mrs. Tremond's trailer, under which he finds

Teresa Banks' owl ring. Agent Desmond only appears in the movie, and he and the trailer itself disappear shortly after he finds the ring. This is the same ring that Laura Palmer wears to compel Bob to kill her.

When Cooper drives to Carrie Page's home in Odessa, Texas, he notices a utility pole outside of her house with the same larger number 6 screwed into it along with the accompanying numbers 324810. He looks up at the distribution transformer on top of the pole and hears electrical humming coming from the lines. Lynch is making a connection here between homes and electrical lines. While the connection is ubiquitous and therefore may seem insignificant—unless you're off the grid, your home is connected to electrical lines—we must remember what Lynch is concerned with in regard to such a connection. It is these electrical lines that bring television shows, and their characters, into our homes.

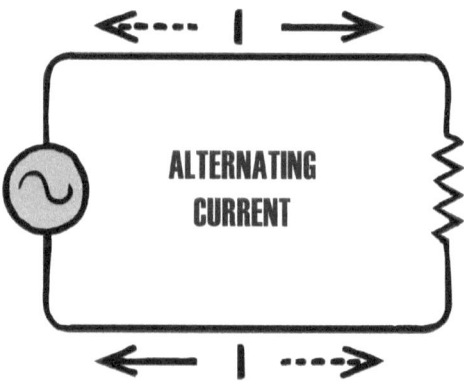

Electricity originates from a power plant in the form of alternating current (AC), which causes the flow of electrons to change direction, switching back and forth and from positive to negative as they travel through power lines along our streets. As video essayist Twin Perfect astutely points out, AC electricity acts as a metaphor for Lynch's "perfect balance of positivity and negativity."[37] This is not just an assumption. Twin Perfect further notes that Lynch himself was not only aware of alternating current, but that he actively incorporated analogies to it into his work. The evidence rests in Lynch's description of his unmade film, *Ronnie Rocket*, which, according to him, "is about a three-foot-tall man with, you know, a red pompadour, a fake red pompadour, who runs on alternating current electricity."[38] Lynch's specificity with respect to the type of electricity on which Ronnie Rocket runs is noteworthy, as it comes from an artist who almost never explained his work, and when he did, his explanations were intentionally unspecific.

It's interesting to note that the alternate title of the screenplay for *Ronnie Rocket* is *The Absurd Mystery of the Strange Forces of Existence*. This, more or less, sums up much of Lynch's oeuvre. In the script, he describes Ronnie's hair as a "red wig of high wavy pompadore [sic] style hair."[39] His hair is wavy because he runs on waves, electrical waves, and he looks like it. The movie is, literally, about electricity. The antagonist, a character by the name of Hank Bartells, has usurped control of the electricity in this world, and as another character Terry says, "He's got the electricity all fouled up, reversed or somethin' so's it's around the wrong way and all the power is suckin' up light...he's making darkness as fast as you can pee your pants..."[40] In the script, the characters control the electricity and it's the electricity that is the key to their survival. In fact, Ronnie's lifeblood is electricity:

Bob and Dan now have the shirt open and they are in the last stages of fitting Ronnie with his electrical chest appliance. This is a life-sustaining device, which Ronnie will have to wear continually. It fits to his chest with little shoulder straps and one strap which goes around his torso. A series of electrical wires come off this device and go surgically into Ronnie's body. One fat cord comes out of the appliance and it ends in a plug.[41]

It is electricity that allows the Tremonds, and the other entities in the Room Above the Convenience Store, to descend "from pure air." David Lynch often spoke of how he generated his ideas. He equated getting ideas to "catching the big fish." The idea appears in your mind, completely at random, and your job as an artist is to catch it and translate it into a communicable medium. An idea arises in your brain when a neuron fires an electrical signal, and thus communicates with other neurons. The idea for *Twin Peaks* started as an electrical impulse in David Lynch's brain, only to be brought to completion in the form of a show transmitted through electrical waves to peoples' televisions inside their homes.

Ideas, stories, characters within the formats of film and television do not exist without electricity. This is the literal case for Ronnie Rocket, who needs to be plugged in every fifteen minutes in order to live, and the metaphorical case for the characters in *Twin Peaks*. Ronnie is fitted with "a life-sustaining device" that fits to his chest with "a series of electrical wires" that connect to his body. While the characters in *Twin Peaks* are not connected to electricity as directly as Ronnie Rocket is, the associations are strong, particularly in the case of Dale Cooper in Season 3, who uses electricity to travel back to his reality through an electrical socket, and who later uses electricity to shock himself out of his semi-catatonic stupor. The entities in the Room Above the Convenience Store also seem charged with electricity; the sound of electrical arcing fills the air as flashes of light spark at times in the background. The Arm, who uses the word "electricity" as a mantra, becomes *The Evolution of the Arm* later in Season 3, whose tree-like branches resemble the dendrites of a neuron, which seemingly pulse with electricity, and whose head is reminiscent of a displaced nucleus.

This room, along with the Red Room, are in-between places. In his interview with Chris Rodley, Lynch remarked, "I like the nowhere part of America. *Eraserhead* is an American film, but it's a little bit in an in-between place."[42] When Rodley asked Lynch if the Red Room in *Twin Peaks* was one of those "places," he responded succinctly, "Yes."[43] When the Arm says, "Going up and down. Intercourse between the two worlds," he is implying that they—the entities that inhabit both the Room Above the Convenience Store and the Red Room—are the conduits between the two worlds—fiction and nonfiction—and they take the operational form of electricity. This makes perfect sense, as it's electricity that connects the world of fiction, in this case the world of television, to the reality in which television viewers live. Furthermore, electricity and its alternating current of positive and negative charges serves as a metaphor for the positive and negative forces that pull us back and forth in our lives. In *Twin Peaks*, Lynch uses this metaphor to examine the interplay between the forces of good and evil.

In the screenplay for *Fire Walk with Me*, Mrs. Tremond responds to the line "Going up and down. Intercourse between the two worlds." She asks, "Why not be composed of materials and combinations of atoms?" This line may seem like a Lynchian non sequitur and, granted, the line did not make it into the movie; however, her question is a legitimate one if, in fact, they are *not* composed of materials and combinations of atoms. If they are characters, symbols of the positive and the negative, rather than flesh and blood human beings, then such a question is apt. Such a question makes sense for the characters in *Twin Peaks* who are self-aware in this in-between world, and thus cognizant of the worlds of fiction and nonfiction that it connects.

Mrs. Tremond's question also speaks to the notion that electricity isn't solely relegated to power lines, that like Ronnie Rocket, it governs the human body, too. Our bodies are composed of atoms that are controlled by electrical impulses. Atoms comprise protons, neutrons, and electrons. Protons possess a positive charge; neutrons, a neutral charge; and electrons, a negative charge. When these various charges become *out of balance* with each other, an atom becomes either positively or negatively charged. The transition from one type of charge to the other permits electrons to flow from one atom to the other. This flow of electrons results in *electricity*. Just as power plants produce and transmit electricity, so do our bodies.

The entities in the Room Above the Convenience store and the Red Room, including the character of Mrs. Tremond, are representative of the positive and negative forces being transmitted from their creators—Lynch and company—to our living rooms. The audience is real, characters are fiction, but there is something that both the people in the audience and the characters they watch share: the forces of good and evil. Both real people and characters confront and experience the same forces. It is these forces that are the constant in both the world of fiction and the world of reality. This is the reason why the names Tremond and Chalfont are featured prominently in this final scene. In the original series, *Fire Walk with Me,* and Season 3, Mrs. Tremond/Chalfont is connected to homes—a trailer, an apartment and a house—that appear to have part of their footing in the world of *Twin Peaks*, and another part in an altogether different dimension. This other dimension, I posit, is our world, where Twin Peaks does not exist as a town, but rather as a television show that is wired into our TV sets. Mrs. Tremond is seen as the gatekeeper of various homes throughout the *Twin Peaks* canon; therefore, it makes sense that her identity would be linked to the gatekeeper of the most important home of the series: the Palmer house.

Alice Tremond, the purported owner of the Palmer house in the Season 3 finale is played by the actual owner of the house,

Mary Reber. Lynch personally asked Reber to play the role, even though she had no prior acting experience. Clearly, the metafictional aspect of the real-life owner of the house being cast as the fictional owner of the house outweighed any concern Lynch may have had with respect to acting ability. Strictly speaking, Lynch wants us to know she is not an actress; he wants us to know that the woman playing the owner of the house *is* the real owner of the house. To know this is to know the world that Cooper has crossed into.

In an interview, Reber was asked why she thought David Lynch "felt it was important to have you, the actual homeowner, play the homeowner in the show?" Reber responded, "I have absolutely no clue, and if you ask him that type of question, which we did, he said: 'That's something you just don't need to know.'"[44] Lynch's non-answer, in a sense, answered the question. He didn't say that it *wasn't* important for the actual homeowner to the play the homeowner in the show; he simply said that it was something Reber didn't need to know. Ostensibly, by skirting around the importance of his casting choice, he seemed to confirm its importance. This is the final scene in the season, if not the entire series, so of course casting Reber as the homeowner was an important choice. Then the question remains: why was it important to cast her?

This question has been largely answered above, but to be succinct, she is a representative of our reality. In our reality, Mary Reber owns this house; in the reality of *Twin Peaks*, Sarah Palmer owns this house. What connects our reality to the reality of *Twin Peaks*? Electricity. Who is representative of electricity? Mrs. Tremond/Chalfont, along with other entities of the Red Room and The Room Above the Convenience Store. The mention of the names Tremond and Chalfont discharges electrical signals in our brains connecting what we're watching to our prior knowledge of *Twin Peaks*.

When Cooper saved Laura Palmer, he didn't just save her from her doomed life, he saved her from the television show itself. There is no show if Laura lives—she must die in order for

the show to survive. Once Cooper steps in and alters the show's storyline by undoing Laura's death, there is no more storyline, and if there is no more storyline, what else is there that exists? While the show may cease to exist, the world into which the show was broadcast remains. Cooper and Laura Palmer/Carrie Page are television characters who are without a home. Not only has Laura been written out of the series, Cooper has written himself out of the series by saving her. Without a murder, there is no reason for the character of Special Agent Dale Cooper to be written to come to Twin Peaks to investigate it.

As Mark Frost has alluded to, *Twin Peaks: The Return* is similar to Homer's *Odyssey*, largely meaning that it's about characters returning home and finding that it's not the home they had been dreaming about returning to. In the case of Episode 18, the two main characters return to a home that's literally not their home anymore. For Laura, this is no longer her house, and for Cooper, Twin Peaks is no longer his town. They have been, essentially, asleep inside a dream—the dream that Phillip Jeffries astutely points out to his fellow cast of characters they're all living inside of—and Cooper and Laura are just waking up to realize it in Episode 18. Frost has mentioned, with respect to Cooper's actions, "...by going back in time and having the hubris to think he could undo something, Cooper was following in the footsteps of Phillip Jeffries. He crossed a forbidden barrier, risked his existential existence to do it, and ended up hurling both he and Laura into a sideways, alternate reality."[45] Frost linking Cooper to Jeffries strengthens the notion that the "alternate reality" that Jeffries found himself in, and that Cooper and Laura/Carrie find themselves in, is opposite of the dream. If one world is the dream, the other is not the dream. The other is our waking reality. Frost doesn't just say Cooper risked his existence; he qualifies *existence*, stating he risked his *existential existence*. While his word choice may seem redundant, Frost is making a distinction between mere survival and survival imbued with meaning. If Laura's purpose in the show is to die, and Cooper's purpose is to solve her murder, the meaning of their lives disappears when Cooper goes back in time and saves Laura's life.

The meaning in Cooper's and Laura's lives is inextricably linked to the television show in which they exist as characters. In Episode 18, when they leave the world of television and enter the world of our reality, they find themselves in a dilemma worthy of the writing of Samuel Beckett. I'm hard-pressed to think of a modern existentialist nightmare as terrible as TV characters that find themselves without a TV show.

Lynch was no stranger to the absurd, and the concept of the absurd with respect to theatre, film, and television is grounded in the futile pursuit of answers in an answerless world. This definition of *absurdism* is reflected quite clearly in those last few moments of Episode 18. The idea of fictitious characters existing in a world of nonfiction is absurd, yet that's what we are witnessing in these moments.

The existential friction Lynch creates between the television world and the real world is palpable, and he references it when Cooper meets Carrie Page. When Cooper offers to drive her to Twin Peaks, Washington, Carrie accepts the offer stating that she needs "to get out of Dodge." While this seems like an offhand remark, and perhaps it is for Carrie, it most certainly isn't for the writers. This idiom, while seemingly ubiquitous, was popularized in the television series *Gunsmoke*. In the show, the sheriff would push unsavory and dangerous characters out of town, telling them to get out of Dodge City or else trouble would find them. Lynch directs his television character to deliver a line made famous by a television show; for all intents and purposes, Carrie is communicating to Cooper through the language of fiction. This reference is also wonderfully ironic, as while most people believe this phrase originated from the fictitious world of *Gunsmoke*, in point of fact, the phrase was derived from the very real, and very dangerous, Dodge City in Kansas. In the late 1800s, Dodge City, Kansas quickly grew a reputation for murder and mayhem, having lacked the structures of law enforcement. In essence, Carrie's use of "get out of Dodge" stems from the real world; however, the reason it became a ubiquitous saying and bears cultural import is because of its use on a television show.

David Lynch and Mark Frost, the writers of one of the greatest television shows of all time, a show that constantly referenced pop culture within itself, were most certainly aware of the connotations of "get out of Dodge" and used it with intention. Of course, it's used to describe Carrie's desire to escape a dangerous situation, but its metafictional purpose is to raise the audience's awareness and prompt them to question: are we watching a television show or are we watching reality? It is this question that Lynch wants us to ponder as we absorb the final minutes of his show.

As Cooper and Carrie stand at the door to Alice Tremond's house, they are looking for answers in an answerless universe. Cooper expects the fictional owner of the house to open the door, but it is the real owner of the house who opens it, and it is at this moment that Cooper must begin to reconcile the merger of these worlds and confront the realization that, similar to Carrie, he has been stripped of his identity in this world. He is not the mystical Sherlock Holmesesque FBI agent that he was once written to be, but rather the anonymous Richard who woke up alone in a roadside motel after a one-night stand. The former is fitting for a television character, the latter is more appropriate for your normal average Joe. Cooper is no longer a television character; he is a nobody asking obnoxious questions at a stranger's door late at night like some traveling salesman.

At times, Alice Tremond speaks to her husband off-screen, and understanding the geography of the house after watching the series, we know he is in the living room. We assume he is watching television, just as she was likely doing along with him prior to opening to door. While we are unaware of what they are watching on television, one thing is clear: they are not watching *Twin Peaks*. If they had been, they would have surely recognized the characters knocking at their door. They're not watching them on television; therefore they do not exist, at least as those characters. The two people at the Tremonds' door are either Richard and Carrie, or perhaps even Kyle and Sheryl, but they do not appear to be Cooper and Laura.

David Lynch often remarked that we're all like detectives in life searching for something at the end of a trail. This sentiment perfectly exemplifies the end of the third, and final, season of *Twin Peaks*. In a literal sense, Cooper is looking for Laura in order to bring her home, as that is what Laura is presumably looking for: home. He attempts to lead her there only to find that it isn't her home—it either was once her home, and now is not, or never was her home to begin with. On a metaphorical level, they are also *looking* for a home, and in this case, the home they're looking for is the home of television, the home to which their characters belong. Instead of their television universe, the trail has led them to their viewers' universe, in which they are strangers in a strange land.

As Cooper and Carrie walk away from the house, confused and dejected, Cooper asks, "What year is this?" This question, on its face, speaks to the nature of time and echoes what Mike asks Cooper in the Red Room in Episode 2 of Season 3: "Is it future or is it past?" Mike asks Cooper this question just prior to Laura Palmer entering the space and approaching Cooper herself. These two questions bookend the season. The season starts with questioning its place in our linear timeline, and it ends in the same manner. The fact that Lynch ends his historic series with a question begs for someone to either answer it, or to leave it alone entirely, as the unanswered question is often more powerful than the answer itself.

It almost serves no purpose to attempt to answer this question. To attempt to answer it is a compelling course of action, and therefore—with respect to the analysis of a David Lynch work—likely the wrong course of action to take. However, a book on the subject of *Twin Peaks* must address it in one form or another.

If Lynch wanted to end his series with a question, we must ask ourselves, how important is such a question? Will an answer to such a question change the lives of the characters on the screen in any meaningful way, or is it merely food for the audience's brains to chew on after the show is over? The episode that precedes Episode 18 is entitled, "The Past Dictates the Future," which may hint at the notion that whatever year the final scene takes place in, it's taking place in the future. However, we can't be sure there is a connection between this title and the final episode.

It seems most appropriate to examine this question through a metafictional lens, as Cooper's crossing over from one reality, the reality of television, to another, the reality of its viewers, is a metafictional journey. TV characters exist inside a medium that is non-linear with respect to time. Whether through the time machine of a VHS tape, downloadable video, or a streaming service, TV characters, at any point in their character arcs, can be summoned by the viewer, their scenes replayed, fast-forwarded, or paused. Through this medium, they are impervious to the repercussions of time and, as a result, live on forever. The question of *what year this is* takes on different meaning when posed in our reality, in which time is linear and impermanent.

Once Cooper and Laura cross over into our reality, they become victims of time. The question, "what year is this," functions as an acknowledgment of their newly realized mortality. In the end, the two characters find themselves in a world that is neither past nor future, a world that's completely new to them: the world of the present. In an interview with Kristine McKenna, Lynch stated, "We live in a world of opposites, of extreme evil and violence opposed to goodness and peace. It's that way for a reason, but we have a hard time grasping what the reason is. In struggling to understand the reason, we find balance."[46] Past and future are also opposites, and while these extremes do not carry with them the moral implications that good and evil shoulder, it is between these two planes of existence that his characters are stuck.

Television characters' lives are written, their pasts and futures printed on the page before the show airs, and exist in a universe in which a question such as "what year is it" is, by and large, irrelevant. The very first time we are introduced to Agent Cooper in the pilot episode, he records into his Dictaphone the time and date: "Diane, 11:30 am, February 24th, entering the town of Twin Peaks." Every time we, the audience of *Twin Peaks*, watch this episode, it is always 11:30 am on February 24th; however, each time we watch it, the time is, of course, different in our world. It is telling that the first words we hear Cooper utter in the series is a date and time, and the final words he utters in the series is a question regarding the year.

Exploring the significance of this final question is, admittedly, a near impossible task. This is, without question, Lynch's intention as an artist. Lynch himself said, "Life is filled with abstractions, and the only way we make heads or tails of it is through intuition."[47] He created images that are meant to be felt, to be understood through intuition, and not over-intellectualized; however, as human beings, the primary way we make sense of such abstractions is to examine them through a critical means. In the above quote, Lynch does unintentionally reveal a clue. He equates the notion of understanding, of knowingness, with making *heads or tails* of the thing. In other words, the path toward understanding his abstractions is through his theme, the balance of opposites, which is the Tao of *Twin Peaks*.

As mentioned previously, in the international version of the pilot of *Twin Peaks*, Bob utters the words, "head's up; tail's up," a phrase that is echoed when Mike asks Cooper for a nickel. Lynch translates his abstractions through symbolism: Mike and Bob are two sides of the same coin.

In *Ronnie Rocket*, the detective character—who is only referred to as the Detective—possesses a rare ability in the story: the ability to stand on one leg. In response to the Detective's unique capacity for maintaining his equilibrium, the character Terry states:

> *People here can't hardly stand up anymore let alone go for a period on one leg, believe me. We do stand on one leg for a moment when we walk. As one foot swings forward on the stride the other remains on the ground and for that moment we are technically speaking on one foot. However, we are in motion, not stationary. The balance is there but are we sure? Because in the next moment the other foot will be on the ground to save us from falling.*[48]

It is notable that the Detective is not assigned a name. It's as though Lynch's intent is to assign the identity of the Detective to us, his viewers, which makes sense because he has time and time again compared his audience to detectives. The fact that the Detective is the only character in the story that can achieve balance deepens the audience's connection to the theme. Just as his characters struggle to maintain balance, his audience must struggle to do the same, constantly changing their perceptions. The ultimate goal is not to reach one extreme or the other, but to achieve an equilibrium between the two opposite states and work to sustain it. At the end of Season 3's final episode, the past no longer dictates the future, as Cooper/Richard and Laura/Carrie ponder the question of time. We can't help but be reminded of the lines, "Through the darkness of future past, the magician longs to see, one chants out between two worlds, fire walk with me!" The darkness of future past has been exposed by the light of the present, and these characters have found their *chance* out.

The Tao is a path, not the end, and therefore it seems fitting that Lynch ends his epic series with a question. Just as Lynch stated, "In struggling to understand the reason, we find balance." It is the investigating, the asking of questions, that lead us to achieve a sense of balance. However, balance is a constant struggle between the opposing gravities of good and evil, as Terry from *Ronnie Rocket* points out: "The balance is there but are we sure? Because in the next moment the other foot will be on the ground to save us from falling." It is our struggle to understand the meaning behind the ending of *Twin Peaks* that ultimately leads to balance—balance between good and evil, past and present, fiction and nonfiction, and ultimately, the opposing versions of ourselves.

When Laura/Carrie hears the disembodied voice of Sarah

Palmer calling out for "Laura" at the end of the Episode 18, she screams Laura's signature scream. This scream, which has become an iconic part of *Twin Peaks*, is followed by the shorting out of electricity, which cuts the power to the house and, assumably, the Tremonds' living room TV set. Her television set is all of our television sets at this moment, signifying the end of the show, the story that has been transmitted to our homes for all these years through the electrical lines. However, while the show is complete, its effect on its viewers remains infinite, as we continue to struggle to maintain our collective balance in this world of light and dark.

EPILOGUE
IT IS IN OUR HOUSE NOW

In *Mulholland Drive*, the Magician on the stage of Club Silencio shouts: "This is all a tape recording. No hay banda, and yet, we hear a band." This proclamation to the sparse audience of a theater speaks to the self-awareness of the film knowing it's a film and sharing that fact with its audience. The characters that Naomi Watts and Laura Haring play function as our proxies in the audience of the theater. They watch as a man playing a muted trumpet takes the instrument away from his mouth while the sound of him playing continues to reverberate in the soundtrack.

A film or a television show is a recording, and as such, has escaped the trappings of time and space. A scene that takes place inside of three minutes on the screen took numerous hours to write, rehearse, shoot and edit; yet, as an audience, we're unaware of this process. Watching a movie or a television show is akin to witnessing a magic trick being performed before our eyes, and that magic trick is the manipulation of time.

David Lynch often compared his job as a director to the job of a magician, as the emotions that are transmitted to the audience through his films and television shows conceal the method of transmission. In other words, magic only works if its operation is invisible. When the Magician in *Mulholland Drive* states, "This is all a tape recording," he is balancing himself upon a narrow wire, as he wants the audience to suspend their disbelief and watch the show (and the movie, which this show is a part of) as though it's reality, while simultaneously acknowledging that what they're watching is not reality, that it is indeed fiction. Not only was David Lynch, as the magician of his worlds, interested in the balance between light and dark—good and evil—but he was also concerned with the balance between reality and fiction. It is this balance that is being negotiated in the final minutes of *Twin Peaks: The Return*.

While Lynch's work may seem enigmatic, particularly the end of *Twin Peaks: The Return*, if we analyze it with respect to its theme, it isn't as ambiguous as it might first seem. The most famous of screenplay gurus, Robert McKee, writes that an "Archplot" is a classically designed story in which "for better or worse, an event throws a character's life out of balance, arousing in him the conscious and/or unconscious desire for that which he feels will restore balance, launching him on a Quest for his Object of Desire against forces of antagonism (inner, personal, extra-personal). He may or may not achieve it."[49]

Twin Peaks, in its television iterations, is rooted in McKee's Archplot. Laura Palmer is murdered, which throws Cooper's life out of balance. Laura Palmer is saved from her death, and subsequently brought back to life, an event that should restore balance to her savior, but it doesn't. It throws Cooper's life even more out of balance, triggering another pursuit to regain the balance that was lost.

Life and death are opposing extremes; exclusively focusing on one or the other will not achieve balance. Balance resides somewhere in the middle of understanding these two states and their symbiotic relationship to one another, and it is within this space that Lynch seeks to guide his viewers. For Lynch, it seems, this grey area manifests itself inside the home. His characters attempt to achieve balance within the home in *Eraserhead*, *Blue Velvet*, *Lost Highway*, *Mulholland Drive* (Hollywood as home), and of course *Twin Peaks*. In *The Return*, the struggle for balance within the home is solidified when Cooper/Richard/Kyle and Laura/Carrie/Sheryl attempt to find it at the door of the Palmer/Tremond/Reber house.

Lynch is examining the reality of our homes versus the fictions we create about them, a notion that is symbolized by the perfect white picket fence, red roses, and yellow tulips that surround a suburban house in the opening of *Blue Velvet*. In the beginning of Episode 1 of *Twin Peaks: The Return*, the Fireman tells Cooper, "It is in our house now," as he references the scratching sound from the adjacent gramophone. The record player should be emitting harmonious music, but instead it produces the sound of damage, of imperfection, of severity, the type of disharmony that can reverberate within a household on an infinite loop. Abuse is cyclical, it's generational, like a record, and when the turntable's needle is stuck in a groove, this sound is destined to repeat itself over and over again.

On the outside, the home is a place of safety, its walls keeping the darkness out; however, on the inside, the house is often the origin of the threat, its walls keeping the darkness in. The home is often two things at once and the balance between these two opposing facets is critical to successfully, or unsuccessfully, living within and maintaining the home.

In C.S. Lewis' *The Abolition of Man*, the author uses the word Tao to describe "the doctrine of objective value, the belief that certain attitudes are really true, and others really false, the kind of thing the Universe is and the kind of things we are."[50] Lewis suggests that every belief system, from secular to religious, adheres to the same core set of values, values that are objectively recognized and agreed upon from one system to the next. This objective reality corresponds to the Tao, which is purported to be mankind's natural design, namely in its predilection toward achieving balance in a world of opposites.

Opposites consume each other while simultaneously sustaining each other. What is left over gets reduced, and what is lacking, gets restored. Balance is not permanent; to understand it as permanent is to misunderstand it. Life is a flow state, and while this seems simple to comprehend, it really isn't that simple. At first glance, in our world and the worlds of David Lynch, life is defined by dualities. The preeminent mythologist, Joseph Campbell, spoke of such dualities and posited that human beings are predisposed to think in terms of opposites in an interview with Bill Moyers:

> **MOYERS:** *Why do we think in terms of opposites?*
>
> **CAMPBELL:** *Because we can't think otherwise.*
>
> **MOYERS:** *That's the nature of reality in our time.*

CAMPBELL: *That's the nature of our experience of reality.*

MOYERS: *Man-woman, life-death, good-evil—*

CAMPBELL: *—I and you, this and that, true and untrue—every one of them has its opposite. But mythology suggests that behind that duality there is a singularity over which this plays like a shadow game.*[51]

Through his mythological landscapes and characters of opposites that inhabit them, Lynch directs us toward transcending these dualities by first recognizing them, and second, merging them together into one. Once we, as an audience, are able to peer through these dualities, and recognize them as not mutually exclusive, we realize we are one with ourselves. Heaven is the state in which we are all connected to, and in harmony with, ourselves, and each other.

It is our goal to achieve this state of equilibrium. It is no surprise that the Red Room was Lynch's favorite part of *Twin Peaks*. It is the "in-between place" where the two sides of one's self can interact and be resolved into a whole.

It is believed that the Tao itself cannot be understood through written language, that it must be experienced in order to be fully grasped. David Lynch created *Twin Peaks* as a means through which to experience the Tao, as watching *Twin Peaks* requires much more from the viewer than simply seeing and listening; it calls for both conscious and subconscious commitments, which allow you to feel the material, as opposed to merely witnessing it. The series and movie require the viewer to *balance* the conscious with the subconscious in an effort to perceive, and touch, the

Tao in its natural and most optimal state.

In Taoism, the goal of practice is to become one with the Tao and harmonize one's will with nature. Lynch dedicated his life to moving beyond duality and achieving oneness through his practice of Transcendental Meditation, therefore it shouldn't be surprising that his work is an extension of this idea, providing a roadmap to his viewers toward achieving the same. The objective of TM is to reach the level of the unbounded, the shared floor of pure consciousness, within which, according to Lynch, happiness is derived. He remarked that negativity—hate, fear, stress—can't live in "the light of pure consciousness,"[52] and he tested this concept each time he shined his lights on his actors and filmed them in their darkest moments. In his work, Lynch is not depicting disturbing moments to frighten us, but rather to cleanse us of the darkness that resides in each of us and direct us toward the light.

It is perhaps fitting to conclude with a dream that David Lynch had, which he discussed at a question and answer session some years ago. A spectator asked him if he had any recurring dreams in his life. He responded, "Yes," and then asked her to come up and stand next to him as he explained it:

"I had this repeating dream. And I'm in the desert and the desert is completely empty and flat and way in the distance, I see my father start walking toward me and there's the heat waves. And I know that I have a good father and a bad father and I don't know which one this is, and he's walking closer and closer and closer," Lynch brought his hand up, his fingers wiggling, "and all of a sudden," he abruptly lunged toward the spectator next to him, surprising her with a shout of "boom!" She reflexively leaped back, visibly frightened by the director's jump scare.

As the spectator attempted to regain her composure, her shock morphing into a type of nervous laughter, the audience began to applaud and laugh as well. Then Lynch added, "and that was my good father."[53]

"The only way you can talk about this great tide in which you're a participant is as Schopenhauer did: the universe is a dream dreamed by a single dreamer where all the dream characters dream, too."

—Joseph Campbell

ENDNOTES

CHAPTER 1

1. David Lynch, interview by Jason Eldredge, *Guest DJ Podcast*, KCRW, June 24, 2009, https://www.kcrw.com/music/shows/guest-dj-project/david-lynch.
2. Chris Rodley and David Lynch, "Billy Finds a Book of Riddles Right in His Own Backyard. *Mulholland Drive*," *Lynch on Lynch* (Revised Edition. New York: Faber and Faber, 2005), p. 287.
3. *David Lynch: Don't fear writer's block, get a set-up, and be patient*, YouTube, David Lynch Collection, starts at 3:33, August 27, 2020, https://youtu.be/uHhf76z6BkM.
4. *A Slice of Lynch*, featurette from the Blu-ray release *Twin Peaks: From Z to A*, (2019).
5. Suzanne Muchnic, "David Lynch's art show: gritty, witty and definitely twisted," *Los Angeles Times*, September 16, 2009.
6. *Ibid.*
7. Emily Petsko, "Inside *Invitation to Love*: *Twin Peaks*' Show-Within-A-Show You May Have Missed," *Mental Floss*, May 29, 2018, https://www.mentalfloss.com/article/546037/twin-peaks-invitation-to-love-show- within-a-show.

CHAPTER 2

8. *A Slice of Lynch*, featurette from the Blu-ray release *Twin Peaks: From Z to A*, (2019).
9. Rodley and Lynch, "Suddenly My House Became a Tree of Sores: A Tale of *Twin Peaks,*" *Lynch on Lynch*, p. 185.
10. Diane Stevenson, "Family Romance, Family Violence, and the Fantastic in *Twin Peaks*," *Full of Secrets: Critical Approaches to Twin Peaks* (Michigan: Wayne State University Press, 1995), p. 76.
11. Rodley and Lynch, "Shadow of a Twisted Hand Across My House. Childhood, memory and painting." *Lynch on Lynch*, p. 10.
12. David Lynch and Bob Engels, *Twin Peaks: Fire Walk with Me*, screenplay, http://www.lynchnet.com/fwwm/fwwmscript.html.
13. John Thorne and Craig Miller, "We're Gonna Talk About Judy— And A Whole Lot More! An Interview with Robert Engels," *Wrapped in Plastic*, #58 (April 2002), p. 8.
14. John Thorne, "The Realization of Laura Palmer," *The Essential Wrapped In Plastic: Pathways to Twin Peaks.* (Texas, 2016), p. 293.
15. David Lynch and Kristine McKenna, "American Pastoral," *Room to Dream*, paperback edition, (New York: Random House, 2019), p. 8.
16. Lynch and McKenna, "People Go Up and Then They Go Down," *Room to Dream*, p. 311.

CHAPTER 3

17. Mark Frost, *Twin Peaks: The Final Dossier*, (New York: Flatiron Books, 2017), p. 133.
18. *Ibid.*
19. *Twin Peaks ACTUALLY EXPLAINED (No, Really)*, YouTube, Twin Perfect, starts at 3:05:50, October 20, 2019, https://youtu.be/7AYnF5hOhuM.

CHAPTER 4

20. J. Robert Oppenheimer, *"Now I become death..."* (video) Atomic Archive. Archived from the original (1965) on May 16, 2008, https://www.atomicarchive.com/media/videos/oppenheimer.html.
21. Walter Wells, "Lust and Longing," *Silent Theater: The Art of Edward*

Hopper, (London: Phaidon Press Limited, 2007), p. 127.

CHAPTER 5
22. Daniel Dylan Wray, "David Lynch on Bowie and the Music that Inspired the New *Twin Peaks*," *Pitchfork*. September 19, 2017, https://pitchfork.com/thepitch/david-lynch-interview-on-bowie-and-music-that- inspired-the-new-twin-peaks/.
23. *Ibid.*

CHAPTER 6
24. Jason Scheunemann, *The Man With the Gray Elevated Hair*, featurette from the Blu-ray release *Twin Peaks: From Z to A*, (2019).
25. American Psychiatric Association. *Diagnostic and Statistical Manual of Mental Disorders, Fifth Edition (DSM-5)*, (Washington, DC: American Psychiatric Publishing, 2013), pp. 291–292.

"Dissociative amnesia is fundamentally an inability to recall autobiographical information that is inconsistent with normal forgetting. It may or may not involve purposeful travel or bewildered wandering (i.e., fugue). Although some individuals with amnesia promptly notice that they have "lost time" or that they have a gap in their memory, most individuals with dissociative disorders are initially unaware of their amnesias. For them, awareness of amnesia occurs only when personal identity is lost or when circumstances make these individuals aware that autobiographical information is missing (e.g., when they discover evidence of events they cannot recall or when others tell them or ask them about events they cannot recall). Until and unless this happens, these individuals have "amnesia for their amnesia." Amnesia is experienced as an essential feature of dissociative amnesia; individuals may experience localized or selective amnesia most commonly, or generalized amnesia rarely. Dissociative fugue is rare in persons with dissociative amnesia but common in dissociative identity disorder.

Dissociative identity disorder is characterized by a) the presence of two or more distinct personality states or an experience of possession and b) recurrent episodes of amnesia. The fragmentation of identity may vary with culture (e.g., possession-form presentations) and circumstance. Thus, individuals may experience discontinuities in identity and memory that may not be immediately evident to others or are obscured by attempts to hide dysfunction. Individuals with dissociative identity disorder experience a) recurrent, inexplicable intrusions into their conscious functioning and sense of self (e.g., voices; dissociated actions and speech; intrusive thoughts, emotions, and impulses), b) alterations of sense of self (e.g., attitudes, preferences, and feeling like one's body or actions are not one's own), c) odd changes of perception (e.g., depersonalization or derealization, such as feeling detached from one's body while cutting), and d) intermittent functional neurological symptoms. Stress often produces transient exacerbation of dissociative symptoms that makes them more evident.

The residual category of other specified dissociative disorder has seven examples: chronic or recurrent mixed dissociative symptoms that approach, but fall short of, the diagnostic criteria for dissociative identity disorder; dissociative states secondary to brainwashing or thought reform; two acute presentations, of less than 1 month's duration, of mixed dissociative symptoms, one of which is also marked by the presence of psychotic symptoms; and three single-symptom dissociative presentations—dissociative trance, dissociative stupor or coma, and Ganser's syndrome (the giving of approximate and vague answers)."

26. David Lynch, "*Lost Highway*," *Catching the Big Fish*, (New York: Penguin Group, 2007), p. 109.
27. Stuart Swezey, "There's So Much Darkness, So Much Room to Dream": David Lynch on *Lost Highway*," *Filmmaker Magazine*, (Winter, 1997), p. 52.
28. Frederick S. Clarke, "*Lost Highway*: The Solution," *Cinefantastique*, (April, 1997), p. 36.
29. Anthony Ferrante, "Obsessive love. Mysterious spirits. Twisted sex. Gruesome murder. *Lost Highway* is David Lynch's strangest trip since *Blue Velvet*," *Film Threat*, (April 1997).
30. Jennifer Lynch, "Entry: August 31, 1984," *The Secret Diary of Laura Palmer*, (New York: Pocket Books, 1990), p. 23.

31. Jennifer Lynch, "Entry: December 16, 1987," *The Secret Diary of Laura Palmer*, p. 111.
32. Jennifer Lynch, "Entry: January 3, 1988," *The Secret Diary of Laura Palmer*, p. 124.
33. American Psychiatric Association *(DSM-5)*, p. 394.
34. *Ibid.*
35. *Ibid.*, p. 291.

CHAPTER 7
36. Clarke, "*Lost Highway*: The Solution," Cinefantastique, p. 36.
37. *Twin Peaks ACTUALLY EXPLAINED (No, Really)*, YouTube, Twin Perfect, starts at 1:11:48, October 20, 2019, https://youtu.be/7AYnF5hOhuM.
38. *Ibid.*, starts at 1:12:04.
39. David Lynch, *Ronnie Rocket OR The Absurd Mystery of the Strange Forces of Existence*, screenplay, http://www.lynchnet.com/rrscript.html.
40. *Ibid.*
41. *Ibid.*
42. Rodley and Lynch, "Shadow of a Twisted Hand Across My House. Childhood, memory and painting," *Lynch on Lynch*, p. 19.
43. *Ibid.*
44. Devon Ivie, "How the Laura Palmer House's Actual Homeowner Ended Up in *Twin Peaks: The Return*'s Final Scene." *Vulture*, September 19, 2017, https://www.vulture.com/2017/09/twin-peaks-laura-palmer-house-real-homeowner-mary-reber.html.
45. David Bushman, "I Just Thought It Would Be Audacious," Conversations with Mark Frost: *Twin Peaks, Hill Street Blues, and the Education of a Writer*, (Ohio: Fayetteville Mafia Press, 2020), p. 271.
46. David Lynch, interview by Kristine McKenna, *Coleccion Imagen*, (Spain: Institucio Alfons al Magnanim, 1992).
47. David Lynch, "*Lost Highway*," *Catching the Big Fish*, p. 45.
48. David Lynch, *Ronnie Rocket* screenplay.

EPILOGUE

49. Robert McKee, "The Principles of Story Design," *Story: Substance, Structure, Style, and the Principles of Screenwriting*, (New York: Harper Collins, 1997), pp. 196–197.
50. C.S. Lewis, "Men Without Chests," *The Abolition of Man*, paperback edition, (New York: Harper Collins, 2001), p. 18.
51. Joseph Campbell, "The Inward Journey," *The Power of Myth*, (New York: Anchor Books, 1988), p. 57.
52. David Lynch, "Light of the Self," *Catching the Big Fish*, p. 98.
53. *David Lynch has a recurring dream...wait for it*, YouTube, David Lynch Collection, July 28, 2020, https://youtu.be/1xhOpcttU2M.

ABOUT THE AUTHOR

William Dickerson is a filmmaker, author, musician, and professor whose work has been recognized worldwide. His debut feature film *Detour*, which he wrote and directed, was hailed as an "Underground Hit" by *The Village Voice*, an "emotional and psychological roller-coaster ride" by *The Examiner*, and nothing short of "authentic" by *The New York Times*.

His first book, *No Alternative*, was declared, "a sympathetic coming-of-age story deeply embedded in '90s music" by *Kirkus Reviews*. His book on filmmaking, *DETOUR: Hollywood - How to Direct a Microbudget Film (or any film, for that matter)*, was called "candidly practical, thoroughly 'user friendly', and an essential instruction guide—especially for independent filmmakers" by *Midwest Book Review*. William is a graduate of the American Film Institute Conservatory, has served on their Alumni Executive Board and was selected by The White House and AFI to serve as mentor to winners of the White House Student Film Festival under two Presidents of the United States.

His writing has been published by *Indiewire*, *MovieMaker*

Magazine, Filmmaker Magazine, The Hollywood Reporter's 'The Wrap,' Script Magazine, Film Slate Magazine, Talkhouse, and *SaveTheCat.com.* He adapted and directed the film version of *No Alternative,* which stars Kathryn Erbe and Harry Hamlin. *The Los Angeles Times* called the movie "a remarkably assured and deeply felt grunge-era coming-of-age picture," and *Film Threat* said it was "a rare indie gem that delivers solidly on all fronts with no missteps." The movie, which was inspired by Dickerson's band from the '90s, won "Best Soundtrack" at the Paris Art and Movie Awards. His band, Saturday Saints (formerly Latter-day Saints), is featured on the soundtrack alongside such musical luminaries as: Mudhoney, Lisa Loeb, Superdrag, Moby, sElf, Failure, Sebadoh, and others. The soundtrack was chosen as one of the official releases of Record Store Day 2019. Saturday Saints are signed to Rhyme & Reason Records on which they released their debut album *Anhedonia.*

William is also an experienced educator, having taught masters seminars and lectured on the subject of filmmaking at schools such as the American Film Institute, Boston University, Emerson College, California State University Los Angeles, and New York Film Academy. He is currently a faculty member at Hofstra University's Lawrence Herbert School of Communication and is the Academic Department Director of Screenwriting and On Camera Performance at AMDA College and Conservatory of the Performing Arts in New York City.

website: *www.williamdickersonfilmmaker.com*
email: *contactwilliamdickerson@gmail.com*

www.ingramcontent.com/pod-product-compliance
Lightning Source LLC
Chambersburg PA
CBHW031414290426
44110CB00011B/372